THE
REALITY TV
HANDBOOK

((((WARNING))))

The skills and strategies taught in this handbook are meant for use by reality stars—who seek to live in multimillion-dollar mansions for three weeks, to let the viewing audience decide whom they will marry, to eat a handful of maggots, to venture to inhospitable locations for weeks on end, or just to help build their careers as actors and actresses. Although all of the information presented in this book is from highly trained professionals, it is presented for entertainment purposes only—in other words, it's not our fault if you get voted out of the house the first week. The publisher, authors, and experts within hereby disclaim any liability from any harm, injury, or damage that may result from the use, proper or improper, of the information contained in this book. Furthermore, we do not assert that the information contained within this book is complete, safe, or accurate for the situation you may find yourself embroiled in. Finally, nothing in this book should be construed or interpreted to infringe or encourage infringement of the rights of other persons or of any state, federal, global, or universal laws, in perpetuity. All activities described should be conducted in accordance with the law—even if your alliance turns against you just before elimination.

—The Authors

THE REALITY TV HANDBOOK

<< AN INSIDER'S GUIDE >>

How to:
* Ace a Casting Interview
* Form an Alliance
* Swallow a Live Bug
* and Capitalize on Your
  15 Minutes of Fame

BY JOHN SAADE AND JOE BORGENICHT
FOREWORD BY EVAN MARRIOTT
ILLUSTRATIONS BY DANIEL CHEN

QUIRK BOOKS
PHILADELPHIA

Library of Congress Cataloging in Publication Number: 2004104630

ISBN: 1-59474-003-8

Printed in the United States

Typeset in Frutiger and Briem Akademi

Designed by Susan Van Horn

Distributed in North America by Chronicle Books
85 Second Street
San Francisco, CA 94105

10 9 8 7 6 5 4 3 2 1

Quirk Books
215 Church Street
Philadelphia, PA 19106
www.quirkbooks.com

CONTENTS

FOREWORD

I signed the contract, got on the plane, and arrived in France. All I knew was that I was going to be on a reality show about dating. It sounded like fun. After all, I'd spent the last year driving a bulldozer for a salary of $18,000, so any money and adventure I could bring into my life had to be a good thing.

Needless to say, what I experienced on *Joe Millionaire* was not at all what I expected.

Being on a reality show is simultaneously the most exhilarating and exhausting experience of your life—it takes a huge mental toll because you're constantly on display (even if you step off camera and into the woods for a little private time, there may be microphones in the trees). Your life is suddenly not your own—the producers reveal your schedule to you only on a need-to-know basis, which means you can never truly relax. In my case, I didn't even know (what I thought was) the complete premise of the show until after I signed the contract! The entire process was like a bizarre summer camp or boarding school experience from which I've both made some amazing lifelong friends and completely changed my life. And I'm grateful for it.

But (you knew there had to be a "but") if I had it all to do over again, there are a few things I'd do differently. Had I been privy to the insider information offered in *The Reality TV Handbook* before going on *Joe Millionaire*, I would have known right from the start what to expect during interviews (see "How to Give an On-camera Interview," on page 58). I would have picked Zora in a less legally binding manner (see "How to

Offer a Nonbinding Proposal," on page 103). And I definitely would have tried to date all of those fantastic women in a more balanced way (see "How to Date Multiple Partners," on page 100).

At the same time, I have no regrets about being *Joe Millionaire*. With the help of my manager, Randy James, I've been able to spin the world's perception of me into a sixteenth, seventeenth, and eighteenth minute of fame. Since the end of *Joe Millionaire*, I've been able to quit my day job driving the bulldozer. I'm playing the world's perception of Evan Marriott for all it's worth. I've done commercials, cameos in feature films, multiple guest roles in several TV series, and hosted a gameshow.

Maybe someday, with the help of the advice offered in *The Reality TV Handbook*, you will be lucky enough to find yourself in a similar position. Take this book with you to an audition, to the island, or to your first nationally televised date. You'll definitely be a step ahead of your costars.

—Evan Marriott
April 2004

INTRODUCTION

Just admit it. You love to watch reality shows. We all do.

Maybe you watch because you like to see the everyday drama of your life played like a game by people just like (but a bit better looking than) you. Maybe you watch because you like to see someone just like (but a bit wittier than) you win a million dollars, a beautiful bachelor/bachelorette's hand, a postshow sponsorship deal, or a (short-lived) career in television. Or maybe you just watch because you love to think that you could do better.

And now, you can.

This book is the bible for reality-stars-to-be. It is the insider's guide for everyone who wants to display his or her ability to manipulate others, fall in love with Mr. or Ms. Right, or just launch a new career in front of a national viewing audience. Whatever your motivation for reality-stardom, *The Reality TV Handbook* is the key to the reality kingdom.

Granted, life as a reality star has its difficulties. The conditions can be rough, the hours long, and your fellow cast boorish. You also risk exposing yourself to ridicule as some of your weakest moments are revealed to the viewing audience. But with this book in hand, you can turn the tables on your competitors. When you know what to expect and how to see the twists coming, you can use the show even as the show is using you.

We spoke with reality-TV producers, casting agents, network executives, relationship advisors, survival experts, psychologists, and even stuntwomen to compile the ultimate guide to securing a spot on the cast; executing a winning strategy; falling in love and getting engaged in three weeks; surviving brutal reality conditions; winning physical and mental challenges; and spinning a reality appearance into a sixteenth minute of fame.

Your first step is to learn everyone's motivation: the players, the viewers, and the producers. Your competitors may be motivated by anything from greed to love to lust to fame. Viewers want to see strong stories and interesting characters. And reality producers want to tell a dramatic story in much the same way as their colleagues who produce dramas and comedies. You've got to know how reality works: how to get on a show, give captivating interviews, wear the microphones and helmet cams, and get clues from the crews. And finally, you must have insight into how to play the reality games.

With this book in hand, your victory may be even closer than you've ever dreamed.

There was a time when prime time television was full of shows featuring the love, betrayal, and eventual victory of actors like Richard Chamberlain or Joan Collins. But today, prime time is full of the love, betrayal, and eventual victory of people just like you. You could very well be one application away from the adventure of a lifetime. As long as you march in with your eyes wide open, your mind fully prepared, and your character fully developed, you may just find what you are searching for.

We all want a happy ending when the story closes. Let the skills that follow lead you there.

CHAPTER 1

GETTING ON THE SHOW

Reality shows want you.

With all of the shows in production, good participants are getting harder and harder to find. To land a spot on a show, you simply need to give the producers what they want, and the following chapter will show you exactly how to deliver.

Character counts in reality television. The genre depends on strong personalities, and producers need to populate the shows with characters the audience feels strongly about—whether that feeling is love or hatred.

The key to getting on a show is to examine all of your strengths and weaknesses honestly, and then use them to define your unique character. The rest is easy. Let your "character" come out in your written application, in your video submission, during the casting sessions, and during interviews with the network.

One warning: Whether you find the show or the show finds you, make sure you know what you are getting yourself into. With so many shows that depend on fooling the participants, it's particularly important that you pay attention to the hints: You *don't* want to end up the subject of an elaborate, nationally televised practical joke.

HOW TO FIND YOUR SHOW

All of your dreams of becoming a reality star hinge on one crucial thing: getting on a reality show. Out of the tens of thousands of reality candidates casting agents process each year, less than 1 percent will actually get on a show. Fortunately, there are ways to improve your odds. Casting directors Sheila Conlin and Katy Wallin, who have cast a variety of reality shows, including *Paradise Hotel* and *Mr. Personality*, recommend research, persistence, and a good phone manner.

1) **Identify which production company is producing the show.**
To find out who is producing your show, begin with an Internet search. Websites like www.sirlinksalot.net and www.realitytvlinks.com, which are devoted to reality shows, should steer you in the right direction. You may also want to read the television industry trade magazines (*Variety*, *Hollywood Reporter*) for further reference. *Do not* waste your time calling the network that will air the show—the person who answers the phone at the network will not know what you are talking about.

((((INSIDER TIP))))

Reality production companies can be cunning from the get-go. A company that produces shows that mislead contestants or have a huge plot twist may change its name before casting its next show. The new name is meant to prevent applicants from knowing what twists they might be in for.

Arrive early to open-call casting auditions. Be prepared for a long wait.

DISCOVER AND BE DISCOVERED

Reality shows find cast members by advertising, recruiting, or appealing to the audience for nominations.

Advertising for Contestants

* Existing shows casting for the next season will post their contact information at the end of the show to tell you how to apply. If there is no direct information on how to apply, record the credits so you can play them back in slow motion. Write down the names of production companies or producers to research more fully.

* Big-ticket shows that have open-call auditions across the country will advertise on local television and radio stations and in the newspaper. Read the daily arts section of the newspaper of the nearest large city. Craigslist.org is also a popular Website for advertising for reality-show contestants.

* Reality shows that are looking for a specific type of person will take a more specialized approach and advertise in trade publications, alumni newsletters, or pamphlets at university dormitories or fitness centers.

Recruiting Contestants

When casting directors are looking for a particular type of person, they may directly approach suitable-looking candidates. In these cases, a casting associate will approach the would-be applicant, explain the show, and ask the person to fill out an application on the spot.

If you are approached by a casting agent, be enthusiastic but keep your cool. People often get overly excited at the mention of a television show, but true reality stars take it in stride. Remember that these agents approach hundreds of people each week, and only a handful of them will make the final cut.

* Popular locations for finding young singles include gyms, beaches, and nightclubs.

* Families are recruited at shopping malls, fairs, and parks.

* Recruiters also frequent urban entertainment districts, sporting-event parking lots, acting improv classes, and major concerts.

Nominating Contestants

Some reality shows (especially makeover shows) need a candidate who fits a very specific profile, but who cannot know that she is going to be on the program. In these cases, the casting department will advertise hoping that someone nominates a friend, coworker, or family member. Sometimes producers will recruit or advertise for candidates and audition them as they would for any other show, but then imply that someone has nominated the person.

((((INSIDER TIP))))

Because so many reality shows have been cast in Los Angeles, most casting associates agree that it is "tapped out" of good contestants, meaning that few good candidates surface during casting calls. While different casting directors have different favorite cities, popular casting stops include Dallas, Chicago, Phoenix, Orlando, and New York. (New York is also "tapped out," but casting calls there generate the most national publicity.)

2) **Contact the production company.**

Be clear with the receptionist—tell him or her that you read the description of the show and would like to contact the casting director. The receptionist should be able to provide you with the appropriate name and number, or you might be forwarded to the office of the producer. The assistant to the producer would then provide you with the information you need to apply.

3) **Contact the casting department.**

Casting departments are staffed with personable people, so the person you speak to will most likely be friendly and informative. He or she will give you further information on applying for the show. As you would in any job interview, ask questions of the casting director or person with whom you speak to show your interest.

((((INSIDER TIP))))

Casting agencies keep files of good candidates, so even if you don't get cast on the show that originally interested you, being friendly and cooperative with the casting representative may help you receive calls for future programs.

HOW TO CREATE YOUR APPLICATION

The first step toward being on a reality show is very similar to the first step to getting any job—filling out an application. Your application is a great way to introduce yourself and demonstrate why you are a perfect candidate to endure hardship or heartache on national television. Applying for a reality show usually involves two submissions—a written questionnaire and a short videotape—that are viewed simultaneously. The videotape is the more important of the two: The casting department is much more interested in how you look and sound than in reading about the trophy you won for most improved player in Little League. Casting directors Sheila Conlin and Katy Wallin, who have cast a variety of reality shows, including *Paradise Hotel* and *Mr. Personality*, give the following tips on catching their eye when you apply.

Making the Video

1) **Use a brand-new tape.**

Production staffs have had hours of unexpected entertainment watching the home movies that remained on the tape after the candidate's application. Unless you have a compelling home movie that might increase your chances of being cast, use a new tape.

2) **Show your living environment.**

Producers like to see where you live—it gives an insight into who you are. Place characteristic items (posters, dolls, books, etc.) strategically but naturally in the background. However, don't focus too heavily on treasured trinkets, pets, or your friends—your dog is not up for a spot on the show.

3)   Get to the point.

Don't start your tape with a long title sequence. Many videotape applications will be viewed only for a few seconds so that casting directors can see what you look and sound like. Make the most of your on-screen time.

4)   Stand close to the camera so that your features can be seen.

The producers are basing their decisions on a gut reaction to you, and so it is critical that your eyes and facial expressions are clearly visible. Wear makeup to cover blemishes if necessary.

5)   Speak loudly.

Choose a background that is free of noise, and speak clearly and loudly, especially if you choose to film outdoors.

6)   Keep it simple.

No need to dazzle with your desktop production abilities (unless you are truly brilliant, in which case you should rethink your career as a reality star). Remember, you are sending this tape to people who are professionals in the craft of making television. They have a staff of professional technicians who have access to much more expensive equipment than you do. You are applying to be a part of the cast, not a part of the crew. Likewise, don't intercut clips from movies or television shows into your tape. As much as everyone loves Mike Myers as Dr. Evil, he isn't going to help you land a spot on the show.

7) **Don't use copyrighted background music.**
If you are selected for the show, the producers will not be able to use your audition tape for a best-of "clips" show without permission from the copyright holder.

8) **Review the tape before you mail it.**
This is doubly important if you record your tape while intoxicated.

((((INSIDER TIP))))

Don't worry if you have to start and stop the camera yourself. Casting agents and producers are accustomed to seeing videos that start with an empty wall or couch, with the subject walking in from behind the camera.

The Written Application

1) **Be long-winded.**
Spend some time with the written application. Download the application from the show's Website (or the Website of the production

company or network if the show is brand new) and type full responses to each question. Don't handwrite the application, and don't answer questions with just one or two words. This is your chance to show the casting agents who you are.

2) **Allow your personality to shine.**
The casting department is interested first and foremost in who you are, and this includes your likes and dislikes. Give honest responses, even if they are abrasive, egotistical, or outrageous.

3) **Mention notable accomplishments from your past.**
Whether you were senior class president, started an Internet company, or went over Niagara Falls in a barrel, the casting agents want to know about it. See "Defining Your Character" on page 24 for further discussion.

((((INSIDER TIP))))

Some applicants believe that they will stand out if they enclose gifts with their applications. Since applicants frequently resort to this strategy, there is no guarantee that the casting staff will remember yours.

4) **Do not enclose naked pictures of yourself.**
Casting agents usually disqualify any application that includes nude photos, no matter how attractive the applicant.

DEFINING YOUR CHARACTER

Most reality contestants are defined by where they are from and what they do for a living. These two elements make a nice, tidy frame for your character, and they have the added advantage of fitting neatly in a text box beneath your name every time you are on camera. You can't escape this categorization, so you might as well make it work for you in your applications and in face-to-face interviews.

* **Sell your job.**

  Use a creative euphemism to play up your current job. If you are a paralegal, say you work in law. If you are a security guard, describe yourself as a security specialist. If you are taking evening classes at a community college, say that you are working toward your pre-med degree. If all else fails, list yourself as a business-man (or woman).

* **Play up any interesting extracurricular activities and hobbies.**

  Adapt your pastimes and previous experience into an impressive descriptor. If you were a member of the Reserve Officer Training Corps (ROTC) in college, describe yourself as a former military officer to sound tough and disciplined. If you teach an aerobics course at the gym, describe yourself as a fitness trainer to emphasize that you are physically fit and sexy. If you know how to snowboard, describe yourself as an extreme-sport enthusiast to convey a youthful spirit and a daring, reckless attitude.

* **Use the new description of yourself to your advantage.** In both your video and written applications—and eventually in your face-to-face interview—mention your occupation every chance you can, both to define yourself and to suggest that you have an edge. The casting department and producers will be very comfortable with assertions like these, and will be grateful that you present a consistent character. For example:

  • "As a security specialist, I've been trained to see what everyone else misses. I can read any situation like a book. I'm reading you right now."

  • "If a career in law has taught me anything, it's to always expect the worst in people."

  • "As a businessman, I survive by thinking on my feet all day long. This is going to be a piece of cake."

HOW TO AUDITION LIKE AN IDOL

All things being equal, if you were given the choice of either starving in a harsh environment for two months with cutthroat competitors or living in Los Angeles and performing before thousands of adoring fans with one sarcastic judge as the lone buzzkill, you would probably choose the latter. If you possess an extraordinary singing voice—and at least a hint of star potential—a performance-based show is the reality competition for you. The odds of landing on this type of program are very long (though if your vocal range and "it" factor are limited, you may earn yourself a spot on the bloopers reel), but by concentrating on what the judges are looking for, you can get the competitive edge. Nick Bedding, an executive at Hollywood Records, outlines the most important elements of a successful audition.

1) **Your song.**

What the judges are looking for: They just want to hear your voice—they are not going to consider the lyrical context or subtle themes of your song.

How you can deliver:

- **PLAY IT SAFE.** Don't get overambitious. Choose a song that is in your range and within your abilities. Many singers hope to get extra points for attempting a very challenging song. They don't.

- **CHOOSE AN UNFAMILIAR SONG.** Avoid popular standards or pop tunes. The judges will have heard these songs thousands of times, and that won't help your chances.

- **PICK A SONG THAT MEANS SOMETHING TO YOU.** You are much more likely to sing from the heart.

2) Your entrance.

What the judges are looking for: Confidence and charm.

How you can deliver:

- **SMILE.** Give the judges every opportunity to connect with you.
- **REMAIN CALM.** Don't be intimidated by the judges. Imagine them naked, or better yet, read up on the judges before you audition, and imagine each of them in the middle of one of their career failures.
- **WEAR REASONABLE CLOTHES.** What you wear says much about you. Stay true to who you are—it's easy to spot someone who is merely wearing a costume, so don't just imitate a new look from a teen magazine. An original (within reason) style will stand out in the judges' minds.

3) Your performance.

What the judges are looking for: First, raw technical ability, followed by originality, execution, confidence, and showmanship.

How you can deliver:

- **SING TO THE JUDGES.** Consider the size of the performance space. Don't bellow as if you are singing the national anthem at a sporting event, but don't sing too intimately, as if you are in a small coffee shop.
- **DON'T MIMIC.** The world already has a Justin Timberlake and a Whitney Houston. The more you imitate a star, the more the

judges are going to compare you unfavorably to them. Remember, their goal is to find the next big thing, not a carbon copy of an existing star.

- **DON'T OVERSING.** Let the purity of your tone do the selling, not fussy vocal acrobatics.
- **DON'T STOP.** If you fall out of key or miss a cue, correct the mistake quickly. Do not ask to start over. Remember, nobody is perfect, and the judges are looking at more than just your technical ability.

Be confident, remain calm, and have fun.

Regaining your composure and not allowing yourself to falter goes a long way toward demonstrating that you have the confidence to be a star.

- **HAVE FUN.** Communicate through your facial expressions and body language that you are having a great time. As long as your technical abilities are solid, enthusiasm will translate into additional points in your favor.

4) Your interactions with the judges.

What the judges are looking for: A sense of your personality.

How you can deliver:

- **BE YOURSELF.** Don't put on an act. If you are yourself, you never have to worry about falling out of character.
- **DON'T CONFUSE ATTITUDE WITH PERSONALITY:** A little attitude goes a long way—usually in the wrong direction.

((((INSIDER TIP))))

Because of the high volume of people auditioning for the show, the celebrity panel cannot critique everyone who applies. Your initial audition will be in front of several producers, who only send through the best, the worst, and the most interesting candidates. If you don't have the musical chops, your next best chance for getting in front of the camera is to be truly awful, with a creative flair.

HOW TO ACE A CASTING INTERVIEW

In the business world, most hiring decisions are made within 10 seconds after you walk into the interview. In the world of reality television, you are judged from the moment you walk into the building. But a successful casting interview is not just a matter of looking good: Your performance under pressure combined with keen observation skills are what will get you to the next level. Body-language expert Patti Wood suggests you read both the waiting area and interview room, while executive recruiter Erica Rutkin Keswin and independent consultant and interview instructor Carrie Leonard provide tips on presenting the "real you."

1) **Act as though your interview starts from the moment you walk into the building.**

    Greet everyone, from the valet to the security guard, from the receptionist to the production assistant who gets you water. Receptionists and assistants are often asked for their opinions, and you want *everyone* on your side. Start conversations with people in the waiting room—you never know where a reality producer will show up to test your ability to be "real."

2) **Project confidence.**

    Walk into the interview like a champion. Offer a firm handshake and a pleasant smile. Make eye contact.

((((**INSIDER TIP**))))

Dress for the interview as the "character" you want the casting agents to see (e.g., a cunning vixen, a country bumpkin, or an arrogant athlete)—they need to be able to visualize you as you will appear on the show. Therefore, unless you are applying to be a mogul's apprentice, don't dress as if you were going to a formal job interview. Be yourself—or your most typecast version of yourself.

3) **Orient yourself in the interview room.**

Face the interviewer(s), sitting slightly at an angle. Face away from direct sunlight or visual distractions like televisions or windows.

4) **Look for the "yes" man or woman.**

In every interview there is a "goodie" person. This person will nod, smile, and generally agree with everything you have to say—you could insult his mother and he would still nod at you. Do not play up to this person. Rather, use him to help you determine who's in charge (see "Finding the Decision Maker," on page 33).

((((**INSIDER TIP**))))

You can determine the size of the role you are auditioning for by the number of interviews you are asked to attend. If you are up for a minor role, you may get by with a single interview with a casting agent. If you are up for a major role, you may go through five or six interviews, moving your way up the chain from casting department to producer to executive producer and finally to the network.

5)   **Listen to and answer questions carefully.**

Take particular care when answering the question, "Why do you want to do this show?" Discuss how you want to "test yourself" or "find adventure," or say that "every other means of searching for love has failed." If there is a prize at the end of the show, it's acceptable to say that you want to do the show for the money, but have a good story to tell about what you intend to do with it.

((((INSIDER TIP))))

Especially with "surprise" reality shows, you may be led to believe you are being cast for one type of show when you are in fact being cast for something completely different. The interview questions may tip you off to the show's true content. Just as the interviewer is trying to get a gut reading on you, you will develop a gut reading on the show. Trust those instincts.

6)   **Engage the interviewers who are "closed off" to you.**

Anyone in the room sitting with his arms and/or legs crossed may be completely turned off by you (especially if he also avoids eye contact and leans away from you in his chair). He may also be testing to see if you engage him. Mention his disinterested posture to show the rest of the room how perceptive you are. However, before doing so, check the orientation of his heart and feet to get a more accurate read. If his heart and lower body face toward you, then he is still engaged in what you are saying—he just may be shy or especially guarded.

FINDING THE DECISION MAKER

Putting your finger on who the decision maker is can be difficult, especially since reality-show interview tactics can be somewhat unconventional. Use the following body language reads to help identify (and play slightly more to) the decision maker.

* **Response checking.** This may be the best tactic you can use to find the decision maker in a room. Others (particularly any yes men) will frequently look at one or two decision makers to evaluate their response to you.

* **Hands to the back of the head.** Someone employing this gesture is a person of power.

* **Seating position.** Don't be fooled into thinking that the person at the head of the table is automatically in a position of power; while this may be true in a conventional job interview, you cannot rely on this tell to give you an accurate read of who is actually in control.

7) **Exit gracefully.**

Watch for clues that the interview is over, and then decisively stand and thank the interviewers for their time. Shake hands with each participant, express once again your interest in the role, and ask about the next step in the process. Ask how long the decision will take and when you should expect to hear back from the production company. Do not get trapped in a long good-bye where you are shaking hands more than twice in your efforts to leave. Leave them with a polished, decisive final image.

HOW TO NAIL THE FINAL NETWORK INTERVIEW

You've been tested, dissected, and analyzed. Detectives have spoken to your ex-roommates. Every ATM withdrawal you've made in the past 10 years has been scrutinized. Only one hurdle remains between you and your dream of starring in a reality-television program: final network approval. You might be able to get on the show without having to appear before the network executives—sometimes the tapes of your past interviews will suffice. However, if the entire series hinges on you, network representatives will want to meet you. Fortunately, the steps for acing the final network audition are easy to learn. The information here is provided by an anonymous network executive.

1) | Don't change a thing.

You've been chosen by the producers because of the person you've shown yourself to be so far in the process. The producers have provided the network with a sketch of your personality. They've described your strong points and what they like about you. Don't surprise (and disappoint) everyone by revealing a heretofore hidden aspect of your personality. By now, your responses to basic questions will sound to you like a "greatest hits" tape, but stick with it. Now's not the time to start revamping.

((((INSIDER TIP))))

Initial interviews are recorded with small, consumer-grade cameras. Later interviews are recorded with professional equipment and will be well lit. If the lighting appears to be professional, you can assume that you are a finalist.

2) Trust the producers.

The producers want you to succeed. They've prepped you on what the network executives are like, what they are looking for, and where they may have doubts about you. Together, you will have worked out a plan to alleviate any doubts about you, and the producers may have even suggested behavioral changes you should make so that you appear stronger or less neurotic. Follow through with these plans.

((((INSIDER TIP))))

When casting directors are considering you for a lead role on a show, they will create an edited version of their interviews with you to share with the network. During a taped interview with a casting person, if you are asked the same question several times (often with additional coaching from the casting director or producer), it may be that he is hoping to get a better "take" of your response to share with the network. You can increase your chances for success by taking the hint and providing a more humorous or poignant answer to the questions posed.

3) | **Don't crack.**

Sometimes network executives may challenge you or ask questions in a way that makes you wonder whether they like you. They may even become verbally aggressive. Don't take these actions personally. Keep your game face on, stay confident, and don't crumble.

BACKGROUND CHECKS

Networks go to great lengths to protect the safety and reputation of all participants. As a reality contestant, you will be examined on three fronts: your background, your medical condition, and your psychiatric condition. Here's what you can expect.

The Basics

Most reality shows hire professional private investigators to conduct a basic research-level investigation of all contestants, including:

* Civil and criminal court records from any states in which you have lived.

* Records from the Department of Motor Vehicles from any state in which you have lived.

* Your credit history.

* An identity search to make sure your social security number matches your name throughout the paper trail of your life. This search would uncover restraining orders placed against you, driving-while-intoxicated incidents, arrests (that haven't been expunged), personal bankruptcies, divorces, and civil complaints. When this information is compared against your application, it may also reveal discrepancies that might warrant further

investigation. The background investigators may also conduct a neighborhood-level inquiry, where detectives interview current and past neighbors, previous employers, roommates, etc., with an eye toward discovering all of your secrets.

Medical Condition

Most shows will require you to take a physical examination, and you will be asked to disclose previous illnesses, conditions, and allergies. It is important that you divulge all items of note at this time—this information will be used to evaluate what games, stunts, or challenges may be unsuitable for you. Strategic disclosure of various "allergies" may give you an edge in certain challenges (see "How to Eat Almost Anything," on page 146.). You will also be asked to take a blood test, and if the show involves overnight activities, you may have to give your consent to be tested for sexually transmitted diseases.

Psychiatric Condition

Almost all reality shows employ a psychologist or psychiatrist. During the application process, she might ask you to undertake the following:

* An MMPI-2 test (a written exam that screens for psychiatric conditions).

* Other aptitude or personality evaluation tests (such as the 16 PF or the Myers-Briggs).

* A one-on-one interview.

CHAPTER 2

STRATEGY SKILLS

Congratulations! You have arrived.

Now that you've beaten the odds and actually secured a spot on a show, it's time to put on your game face—even before the cameras start rolling. The earlier you establish your character with the other people on the show, the better.

The beauty of reality TV is that it is a mirror of our everyday, real-world adventures compressed into 13, one-hour episodes. With a little knowledge of the way people work—their motivations, their personalities, and their ability to manipulate—you can increase your chances of becoming the puppet master. Those who play strong and loud at the outset generally become known as "the first one eliminated," so enter the game carefully. Create alliances early, but stay under the radar for the first few days so that you can observe and connect with your potential teammates. Once the game is under way, manipulation is the key. Whether you're playing your competitors by displaying emotion on cue, using alcohol to gain information from your fellow reality stars, or working to eliminate your enemies, you've got to be quick on your feet if you want to pull the strings quietly. The true puppet masters, of course, are the producers and other professionals who are working to create a ratings-worthy story—and as a result, you'll have to know how to play them, too.

Remember: Play the game with your opponents. Play the story with the producers. And play the drama for the viewers. Before long, no one will be able to get enough of you.

HOW TO FORM AN ALLIANCE

There is strength in numbers. The problem is, on a reality show you can't trust your numbers, or even let anyone else know that your numbers exist. Whether you're imprisoned in a house with a dozen other competitors, stranded in an inhospitable, far-off location, or working to find a backstabber who's out to foil your success, your best bet for victory is a strong alliance. But plan your moves carefully, and remain noncommittal until you get a sense of what motivates your competitors. Management trainer Suzanne Gooler and social psychologist Dr. Jonathan Butner recommend lying low, bonding with everyone, then . . . allying to conquer.

1) | **Blend in.**

Focus on acting even-keeled. Take note of the quietest member of your team, and say just a bit more than she does. Allow someone else to lead a team or be a project manager, even if you think you know better. This way, you can silently observe your team members to determine who you will want on your alliance, and you will not be voted out of the game early for posing a threat.

((((INSIDER TIP))))

When you first start the show, save most of your commentary for confessional interviews. Play to the producers' sense of storyline by giving them material to edit. Make one or two absolute claims, such as, "I have already won," or "These people have no idea what I'm capable of." You'll allow the producers and editors to start setting you up as a real contender.

2) **Get in the trenches.**

Work alongside your teammates in every aspect of cleaning, cooking, building, maintaining, and providing for the house or camp to cultivate credibility and gain the respect of your teammates. This will put you in a position of authority.

3) **Identify those with whom you want to form an alliance.**

See "Choosing Your Allies" on page 44 for tips on determining who will bring you the most success.

4) **Bond with your teammates over the mistakes of the team's first leader.**

No one likes working for "the Man." Identify your current leader as such, and connect with your teammates over how much you hate dealing with his dictatorial style.

5) **Determine the goals of each member of your alliance.**

Establish what each individual's goals are both within the game and the outside world. Begin a casual, personal conversation with every individual to uncover what they do for a living, what they like or don't like about what they do, and what they hope to accomplish both on and after the show.

6) **Paint the big picture for your potential allies.**

Use the personal information you've gathered to show each individual what's in it for her. For example, if your teammate is looking for exposure (to advance a career in film or television), tell him or her that your alliance will be the strongest, most dramatic, and thus, most recorded. Remember that whatever the goal, people are generally driven by power, money, and/or exposure.

7) **Manipulate your allies into thinking that the alliance was their idea.**

Alliances are strongest when they are created by choice. Rather than telling or asking a person to join your team, let your potential alliance-mates think that they have created the coalition. Suggest that you would be happy to join them in their efforts since your goals match closely. To create the sense that they are playing you, use phrases like, "like you just said," or "what you said is so true, that . . . ," whether they said it or not. Unless you're on the attack, people usually won't deny that they said the words you're putting into their mouths, particularly if the statements you're crediting them with are wise or witty.

How to Maintain an Alliance

1) **Create informal opportunities for teammates to share a story that indicates something about themselves.**

Focus on building the team from a personal foundation. Spend time together in informal activities around the pool, suite, or camp to bring your alliance together on a personal level.

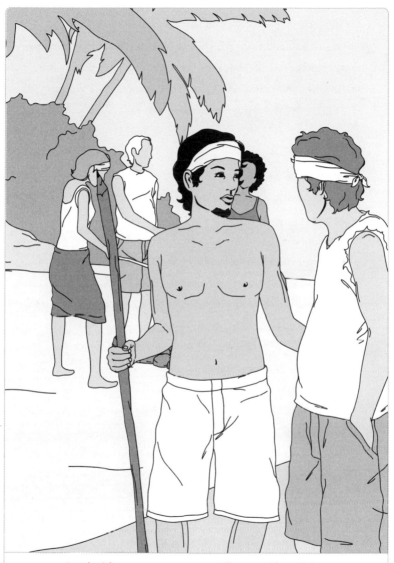

Bond with your teammates casually to avoid suspicion.

CHOOSING YOUR ALLIES

As much as you will want to work with agreeable, similar people, the best strategy when building an alliance is to look for a diversity of strengths and abilities. As leader, you should have the strongest social and political skills. Add members with the following abilities:

* Physical strength.

  Choose a teammate who will be able to win any physical challenge set before him or her. This will increase the chances that at least one alliance member will win either the reward or exemption challenges (and share the benefits with you).

* Emotional strength.

  Someone who has effective relationship skills but who lacks the self-confidence and authority that you possess can communicate effectively with other alliance members and your opponents. He or she should be able to appeal to people's emotions.

* Following strength.

  Include one teammate who will take your direction and ultimately become your closest ally. You will make him believe that your only goal on the show is to support him so that you can win together—when in reality, the loyalty will be reversed. Your follower will believe that he is in charge of the alliance, when in fact you will be leading the charge.

2)   **Recognize and reward strengths and contributions.**

Be clear and specific about each individual as you publicly reward his or her contribution. Use phrases such as, "Thank you, Lisa, for fixing us all peanut-butter sandwiches tonight," or "Thank you, Michael, for gathering all that firewood—we ought to be able to build a big fire to keep us warm tonight." Share any rewards you win accordingly and for specific reasons.

3) **Open yourself up to your allies.**

You want your alliance to have a common vision and a common purpose—yours. As a result, you must encourage your allies to feel as if they know you personally. Offer an extra dose of vulnerability by taking responsibility for someone else's mistake. Such "selflessness" will generate respect for you as a leader. However, don't take too many hits, lest you wind up taking the fall as well. Use this strategy sparingly, particularly when flying under the radar (see "How to Fly Under the Radar," on page 47).

4) **Use information strategically.**

Information is power. Initially, share as much information as possible to build loyalty, trust, and your position on the team. As your alliance grows deeper, communicate changes only with those members who are closest to you.

((((INSIDER TIP))))

Choose a name for your alliance. The simple act of naming your group, team, or alliance creates an "us versus them" mentality. Your group will see outsiders as dissimilar and not as smart, and will attempt to dole out more punishment to those not in your group.

DETERMINING LOYALTY

Use the following test to determine whether a person in your group is more allied to the group or to himself:

1) Make one bracelet for each teammate. All but one of the bracelets should be exactly the same. The one that is different should be noticeably, but not garishly, so (a different color or a different weave).

2) Approach each group member in private. Offer each teammate the choice of a bracelet. Be sure to tell your teammate that you made one for everybody. If your teammate selects one of the similar bracelets, then she is most likely focused on the team. If your teammate selects the unique bracelet, she is most likely focused on a personal agenda.

3) Replenish the unique bracelets as necessary, and continue until each teammate has made a selection.

HOW TO FLY UNDER THE RADAR

Taking the quiet path toward victory can be just as successful as manipulating the team as the alpha dog. Lurking in the background can be an excellent position from which to observe other contestants and gather evidence while remaining safely out of the line of fire. Masters of flying under the radar stay in the game until the very end—when no one has even given them a second glance, because their threat factor is zero. Others will dip in and out, switching between playing the role of the quiet, supportive benchwarmer and the vocal team leader. Here's some advice on how to stay on the sidelines all the way to the final round. But be careful—management trainer Suzanne Gooler notes that if your allies begin to question your ability, it's time to step up and prove yourself.

1) **Do just enough to avoid causing problems.**

   If you have chores, quietly go about your business. Let others complain about the work, the leaders, or the players who sleep all day.

2) **Avoid letting others into your personal life.**

   Do not discuss your homesickness or your family or friends. If others want to talk, listen, but add just enough of your own information to avoid appearing aloof or uncaring.

3) **Be agreeable.**

   Let others make the decisions even if you have a conflicting opinion. Do it their way to show that you are still useful.

Remain neutral while others argue in public.

4) **Take a safe, neutral position during arguments in the house or camp.**

Allow others to passionately attempt to resolve issues or raise their voices to make a point. Remain disengaged, and go with the flow.

5) **Be as physically unassuming as possible.**

Hunch your shoulders, avoid making eye contact, sit down when people talk to you, and retreat to the back of the line during group activities. All of these cues will silently communicate to others that you are not a threat, which will certainly work to your advantage as they vote off stronger or more opinionated characters.

HOW TO MANIPULATE YOUR COMPETITORS

The "rules" of human social behavior may not be fail-safes on a reality show, but they most certainly give you an edge toward victory. Humans have thousands of bits of information to process every second of every day. No one has the time or energy to stop and analyze each piece of information to determine its validity. As a result, people rely on a series of shortcuts that social psychologists have studied—and reality winners have often used and abused. Social psychologist John Butner provides the basic framework of how to manipulate others to get ahead.

1) **Give—and accept—favors.**

While it is a common belief that it is better to be owed than to owe, both positions can be helpful as you work over your competitors. Performing favors for others, even when they don't ask you to, will make them feel obligated to you until they can repay your kindness. Additionally, when others do favors for you, they feel as though you owe them; as a result, they will keep you around as an asset.

To take advantage of human nature, perform a favor for someone—whether they asked for it or not—and then immediately request reciprocity. For example, you might say, "Here, I just made you a cocktail. Now let's talk about who we're going to vote off the show."

2) **Use peer pressure.**

In any group setting, if the majority believe or behave in a certain way, then the other members of the group are more likely to go along with it.

Convince individual allies that everyone else in the group is going to behave in a specific way, and they will affect each other in turn. This strategy can be applied behaviorally as well—when several people perform the same task (such as cleaning the house, building a shelter, and so on), others feel pressured to participate as well.

3)   Convince others that you are an authority in a useful skill.

In a group setting, individuals tend to believe, trust, and rely on those who are in charge. To be *perceived* as an authority is almost as powerful as *being* an authority.

Talk about—or execute—your particular expertise every chance you get. Your team will begin to see that they need you to survive or get along.

4)   Convince your competitors that you are indispensable.

People determine value by determining scarcity—if there are fewer of something, then it *must* be valuable. Put this concept to work by convincing others that you are the only one who can prepare or provide food, or by convincing a bachelor or bachelorette that you are the *only one* who can perform a certain task (e.g., understand him, make him happy, treat him well on birthdays and anniversaries).

5)   Tell your competitors that they are like family.

People's thresholds for familial conflict are much higher than they are for friends. Tell a strategic ally that she reminds you of your sister, daughter, or mother. Just making such a statement will both create a deeper subconscious loyalty and cause your ally to think twice about doing you harm or holding a grudge against you.

How to Lie—and Get Away with It

When you lie, particularly to your allies, you risk your own credibility and the hostility of your team. As you lose their trust, your allies will put less energy into the alliance and more into their own agendas. If you feel you must lie for your own survival, use the following guidelines for getting away with it.

1)　**Keep most of the facts in your story accurate, but change a small portion to fit your deceit.**

People tend to recall only about 60 percent of what they are told—and the 60 percent that they do recall tends to be the dramatic. Make your lie the dull part of your story.

2)　**Keep your story straight.**

Ideally, you will be able to memorize your lies. If you doubt your memory, write down the lies that you tell and store them in a safe place, referring back to these notes as necessary. However, understand that this is extremely risky, since your fellow contestants may find this evidence (especially if they are in some way tipped off to its existence by the producers).

3)   Don't allow yourself to feel guilty.

Keeping track of your artifice is important, but stay focused on the game rather than the guilt you may feel. Never think about the viewing audience—you are in the game to win.

4)   If you do need to tell a lie to regain the sympathy of your teammates, tell it in such a way as to increase your stature as a martyr.

For example, "I could not succeed in the challenge because my sister, who was a triathlete, lost her leg in a similar challenge and I can't believe that I've had the mental strength to participate in everything I already have." However, you can only be a martyr once, so save the big lie for as late in the game as possible.

5)   When confronted with a lie, deny it.

While the viewing public may know that you lied, take the chance that your teammates may not have any proof.

6)   If your teammates won't let it go, own up to it . . . with an explanation.

People have an easier time swallowing a lie if there is a reason behind it. Often, just adding the word "because" to your confession will make a difference—for example, "I lied about who I was going to ally with, *because* I was scared." Own up to the lie, but in doing so attempt to explain your position to your opponent. Do not act defensive during this explanation.

HOW TO DISPLAY EMOTION ON CUE

The ability to cry, faint, act dumb, or look scared on cue will prove invaluable when it comes to outplaying your slow-witted opponents. Crying at just the right time disarms any enemy who is out for you. A well-timed faint can put you into the role of victim, create a distraction when events are turning against you, and cast an appropriate pawn into the role of hero. Adopting a dumb or scared persona may just give you a convincing strategy as the rest of your opponents underestimate your every move. Here's how to fake your way to victory, according to acting coach Drucie McDaniel.

Act Frightened

Use this tactic sparingly but directly after a dramatic confrontation or vicious elimination.

1) Consume a large quantity of caffeine (if caffeine is available) to make your hands jittery.

2) Stick one finger down your throat to activate your gag reflex and sweat glands to make your hands clammy.

3) Tighten your jaw and all your facial and neck muscles. Tensing these muscles will also constrict your vocal cords, giving you a strained voice.

4) | **Assume a rigid posture.**

Straighten your back and hang your arms stiffly at your sides.

5) | **Become quiet and withdrawn.**

Cry

Honestly delivered tears often bring others' defenses down. Use the following technique to get close to your enemies right before you deliver your own strategic sucker-punch or to buy a bit more time.

1) | **Apply salt water or sand to the corners of your eyes to make them water.**

Carry a small amount of salt water or sand at all times, just in case.

2) | **Breathe faster and more shallowly.**

Run in place for several minutes so that you are taking raspy, ragged gulps of air. The exercise will also give you a blotchy, flushed complexion. However, you must be careful that no one witnesses your activity.

3) | **Constrict your vocal cords and stutter as you speak.**

4) | **Cover your face with your hands, look away, bite your lip, and put your head down on a table or tree stump to appear as if you are trying to compose yourself.**

ACT FRIGHTENED.

wide eyes

tight jaw

rigid shoulders

CRY.

salt water

hands cover face

FAINT.

eyes closed

relaxed body

target

PLAY DUMB.

wide eyes

drop jaw

hunched shoulders

Faint into Someone

Fainting is the perfect way to foil a bachelor's poolside hook-up or to stop an angry confrontation.

1)   Take a deep breath and gasp for air.

2)   Roll your eyes back into your head.

3)   Buckle your knees and let your body relax completely.

4)   Droop your head forward and crumple your body slowly to the ground.

5)   Reach out or lean into your target as you are falling. He will be instantly distracted from whatever action he was about to take.

Play Dumb

You must begin to play dumb early on for this gambit to be believable. Use this technique to fly low, low under the radar.

1)   Make yourself look smaller.
Hunch your back and shoulders and look down frequently. A lower physical level is frequently perceived as a lower power level. The enemy may dismiss you as nonthreatening.

2) | **Let simple things appear to amaze you.**

Open your eyes wide and drop your jaw to demonstrate astonishment at the simplest notions.

3) | **Chatter incessantly about mundane matters.**

Talk about the weather and its effects on your hair, the water and its effects on your skin, or hermit crabs and the way they skooch from side to side.

4) | **Use nonsense or filler words in every sentence.**

Pepper your chatter with words like "like," "really," and "whatever," and with nonsense words like "irregardless" and "ironical."

5) | **Change the topic of conversation often.**

Do not appear to focus on any one thing. Allow yourself to be interrupted or let your voice trail off before you're finished making a point.

6) | **End your sentences with an upward inflection.**

Raising your tone in such a way makes even declarative statements sound like questions, implying you are not sure of anything.

HOW TO GIVE AN ON-CAMERA INTERVIEW

The interviews in which contestants explain their actions or thoughts are the connective tissue of reality shows. Producers use them to set up a scene, connect the dots in a story, or (most important) get inside a character's head to see why she did what she did. These interviews are your moment to tell the story you want to tell. Producers want good sound bites from you, but sometimes they want more—they need emotional responses for the storyline they're crafting to make a dramatic television show. They might want you to appear to be angry, paranoid, emotionally overwrought, or just plain crazy. Here are a few techniques used in news interviews and strategies culled from producers (who prefer to remain anonymous) describing how they might turn you from sane citizen to reality monster.

1) **Exhaustion.**

   Producers' strategy: Exhaustion and alcohol are two tools producers use to loosen your tongue.

   Your strategy: Provide inarticulate responses. If you are feeling groggy from a lack of sleep or chatty from too many cocktails, put the brakes on. If the producers need something from you, they will come back and ask again later, when you are feeling fresher.

2) **Mind games.**

   Producers' strategy: A producer will ask a line of questions specifically to play with your head. On dating shows the producers might try to lead you to believe that someone is falling for you, or worse, to make you jealous. On strategy shows, the producers may try to make you believe that an alliance is forming against you, or that someone has discovered your plan.

Your strategy: Though you will be starving for information, *you must never believe anything a producer says to you during an interview.* You should respond to questions based on facts you are sure of, and deflect questions based on information provided by the producer. Also, do not play along with "what if" questions, which are also designed to plant doubts in your mind. For instance, "What if Johnny is lying to you?" or "What if Mary chooses someone else?"

3) Mimicry.

Producers' strategy: Knowing that they are facing a lonely, exhausted contestant who may have just experienced an extremely emotional event (for instance, you were just eliminated from the show), the producer may present an extremely sympathetic face. By sharing your pain, and even tearing up on your behalf, she will force the same reaction in you. Conversely, in a different situation, the producer may question you aggressively, baiting you to answer in a much harsher tone than you intended.

Your strategy: This is one of the hardest traps to avoid. It is natural to "mimic" the tone of a person in a conversation (in this case the interviewer), but keep your cool. Remember—the producer is not going to be on camera, you are.

REALIZING THE DEFINING MOMENT

The experience of being on a reality show is so intense, and the psychological stimulation is so severe, that every contestant finds himself reacting to a situation or another contestant in a manner he never could have imagined in "real" life. These reactions often lead to your "defining moment," the scene the producers will high-light and replay as they tell your story. For example:

* You are a virgin in the big city for the first time and you spend the night with a woman. You just became the "fallen virgin" character.

* Normally mild-mannered, you blow your top when you feel another contestant has betrayed you. You are now the "hot-head" character.

* You unexpectedly break down and cry in an interview when describing how you feel about another contestant. You are now the "emotional" character.

Listen carefully to the questions that you are asked in your interviews for hints on how you are being perceived, and gradually own your character, making the best of the situation by showing your sense of humor about the transgression. For instance, if you have come across as a hothead, occasionally respond to a question with good-natured "outbursts." If your defining moment was an awful drunken dance, humorously repeat your moves at an appropriate moment.

((((**INSIDER TIP**))))

While you're in the interview, you're in the driver's seat. Don't finish a thought that is starting to head south. Instead, "bust the take" (stop talking, or talk directly to the interviewer), and then start again with the clean line you want to deliver.

4) **Line feeding.**

Producers' strategy: A crafty producer may get the response he wants by indirectly feeding it to you in the question. For instance, the producer might ask, "When Julia took credit for your work, how badly did you want to rip her throat out?" Because the producers

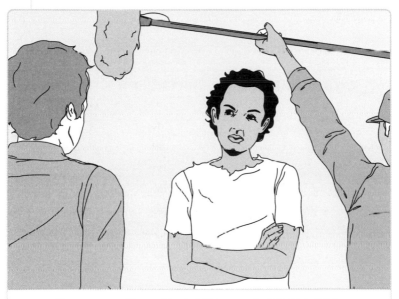

Keep your cool to avoid mimicking a producer's angry tone.

have trained you to answer every question as a sentence, your natural impulse will be to respond, "When Julia took credit for my work, I wanted to rip her throat out. I couldn't believe she did that."

Your strategy: Allow a moment to pass after each question. Make sure you understand what the producer is asking, and respond in your own words.

((((INSIDER TIP))))

Move back from the camera if it is too close—extreme close-ups make you seem paranoid. Sit up or raise your chair so that the camera is at eye level—above eye level makes you look weak.

HOW TO USE ALCOHOL TO YOUR ADVANTAGE

As you think back on your favorite reality-TV moments, it's safe to say that alcohol will have played a role in at least half of them. Drinking can transform a dull conversation into a raucous argument; it can cause two people who barely like each other to become passionate; and it can help provoke a mildly emotional woman to cry hysterically. Producers let the drinks flow freely on most reality-show sets. The viewer may not always see the glasses and the bottles, but they are definitely there, and most contestants are more than happy to imbibe. Producer Kathy Wetherell has witnessed many intoxicated evenings and shares the following insights.

1) **Suggest that everyone share in a toast.**

Whatever the occasion, whatever the time of day, recommend that it is the perfect time for a drink to celebrate something (say, your mother's birthday, the thrill of being on a reality show, or simply the opportunity to be with the "best group of people you've ever met in your life"). Distribute glasses and pour the alcohol yourself so that you can control the amount everyone receives. Top off glasses as soon as they are emptied. Hold back on your own drink.

2) **Suggest a round of shots to further the celebration.**

Once everyone is starting to feel a little tipsy, circulate a tray of shot glasses and a bottle of tequila. Keep your energy level up to get everyone excited. Once the tequila shots have been distributed, the

Control the flow of alcohol.

momentum of the alcohol will build, and the group will be well on its way to drunkenness. Refrain from drinking too many shots yourself.

3) **Offer to refill everyone's drinks.**

Tell everyone you'll get the next round. When you go to the bar, pour yourself a sparkling water in a tumbler or a tonic with a twist to pace yourself and stay safely sober while still appearing to drink with the rest of the crowd. At dinner, considerately top off your tablemates' wine glasses. Splash a little into your own glass for appearance's sake, but only after everyone else's glasses have been filled. This will also help you be perceived as polite.

((((INSIDER TIP))))

If you are not a drinker and your sobriety isn't a cornerstone of your character, disguising your abstinence from your fellow contestants is a wise strategy. Nursing a tonic water with ice and a twist or just holding a beer bottle will allow you to fit in without attracting undue attention.

4) **Mimic the behavior of the others.**

As the drinks begin to flow, mimic the behavior of those who are more intoxicated than you. Laugh, dance, and joke along with the others, but keep your eyes open. As the evening progresses you will find opportunities to play your relative soberness off of your competitors' tipsiness.

5) **Use your competitors' drunkenness to gain information or push them to look foolish.**

On a relationship show, you might suggest that your fellow contestants "showcase" their dancing skills by performing for the bachelor or bachelorette. On a strategy show, you can bond with your enemies and then press for valuable information about alliances or mistakes they have made in the past. Do what the producers do and listen carefully to the conversations around you. Many a budding relationship or secret alliance has been discovered through sloppy mistakes caused by inebriation.

((((INSIDER TIP))))

When available, champagne is the perfect drink for disguising how much you are actually drinking. Pour your own glass quickly; you will only be able to fill it half-way because of the effervescence. Fill the other glasses more carefully, pouring the champagne against the side of the glass, so that your housemates receive considerably more alcohol.

HOW TO MANAGE YOUR ENEMIES

No matter how compassionate and friendly a person you are, on a reality show you will have enemies. Identify and keep your eyes on them early on. You will need an alliance to eliminate an enemy effectively (see "How to Form an Alliance," on page 40). However, as a general rule, stay close to your enemies to ensure your position. Management trainer Suzanne Gooler reminds you that under no circumstances should you become your enemy's enemy.

1) Pretend to be your enemy's friend.

Regardless of the characteristics your enemy puts forth to you, continue to behave as if you are her ally. Ask about her personal life and talk about your own. Back her up if she is being confronted by another player.

2) Ignore your enemy's bad behavior.

Do not confront your enemy when you are set up or lied to. By continuing to be nice to your enemy, you will cause her to believe that you can be duped easily. As a result, she won't see you as a threat.

3) Remain in close proximity to your enemy.

The closer you stay to your enemy, the more you can learn about her plans. Offer to become your enemy's assistant—by doing chores or by helping in other ways.

A carefully placed candy wrapper can sabotage your enemy.

4)   **Quietly sabotage your enemy's endeavors.**

- Steal another contestant's personal belongings and place them in your enemy's sleeping space or personal luggage.
- Prepare a fishing rod for her with the hook tied in a loose knot.
- Steal some food or water rations and leave behind a small personal item of your enemy's as evidence.
- Privately insinuate to one of the judges that a competitor is cracking under the pressure and wouldn't be able to handle the attention that would come with winning the show.

5) | Involve the producers.

Approach a producer and, without saying so directly, imply that your enemy harassed or threatened you, physically or otherwise. Be vague. While you may not have evidence to support your claim, the suggestion may be enough to sway a producer's perception. The producer may, in turn, investigate your enemy with the other contestants, and such questioning, when combined with your work as a saboteur (see step 4), will help to sway others' opinions and allow you to build an alliance against her.

6) | Point out your enemy's errors to your coalition, and eliminate accordingly.

((((INSIDER TIP))))

As you work over your enemies, remember that the ultimate jury will be the home audience. Make a convincing case for why you dislike your enemy to your allies and in your interviews with producers. The more dramatically you outline your issues and justifications, the greater the chance that the storyline will be included in the show, with you playing the sympathetic role.

HOW TO MAKE THE MOST OF LOSING

Losing gracefully on a reality show is very much like losing gracefully when playing Candy Land with an obnoxious preschooler: Be polite, extend congratulations, and move on, hopefully having learned a lesson or two. That's easy enough. However, before you act, think back to your original motives for appearing on the show. Sure, the money was important, but some small part of you wanted to be noticed, make a splash, and find some fame. Don't turn your back on that goal now, just because you've lost. Public relations guru Curtis S. Chin suggests that losing badly can be an excellent means of winning attention.

1) **Play up the shock.**

When your gig is up, don't nod sadly as if you were expecting to be eliminated. React with shock, and even anger.

2) **Storm off.**

Quite often, reality shows allow losers to say good-bye to those who remain. You will make a much greater impact by leaving in a huff. Make your face red by clenching your teeth and holding your breath—this will help punctuate your anger.

3) **Walk back in.**

Turn on your heel and march right back in. If other contestants voted for you to leave, shout at the group. If one person in particular is responsible for your leaving early, create a one-on-one verbal con-frontation. Heatedly demand an explanation. Angrily restate why you are superior to those who remain. Alternatively, lie on the ground and refuse to move. Stay there until security is called to haul you away.

4)   Continue your diatribe during the wrap-up interview.
Use your postshow interview to change your message: Transition out of anger and into boasting. Suggest that the game is rigged against players as strong as you. Say that you posed a threat to the group, so the weak ganged up on you. If applicable, imply that you would not have accepted a marriage proposal from the show's star anyway.

To make a lasting impression on the home audience, make a scene if you're eliminated.

CHAPTER 3

RELATIONSHIP SKILLS

All's fair in love and war. And on relationship shows, both are in play. Nowhere else but in reality-show dating is it acceptable and even expected to meet the perfect man or woman, fall in love, and get engaged in a three-week period. Relationship shows also offer the common Joe the chance to woo the previously un-woo-able, and the common woman the potential to bag the (albeit uncultured) multimillionaire. The possibilities are endless, but only if you know how to play to win.

You have to be able to read a bachelor or bachelorette's body language to know what's really under the surface. Once you find that special someone, a clever escape from the prying ears of the microphones or a carefully orchestrated on-camera rendezvous can provide you with just what you need to make your love a reality. If you're the lucky one making the decisions, then you've got to know how to multitask: the difficulty of dating 25 beautiful people at the same time is compounded by the fact that they're all living together and comparing notes.

When all else fails, you can rely on the fact that if cupid doesn't come to your aid, a well-designed plotline will. Overall, remember everyone's motives: Your love interest is looking for a fairy tale, your producers are looking for an opportunity to blur some on-camera footage, and you—well, only you know your true motivation. And you should keep it that way, at least until the ring is on your finger.

HOW TO READ A BACHELOR OR BACHELORETTE'S BODY LANGUAGE

Making it to anywhere near the final elimination round on a dating reality show involves much more than just falling (quickly) in love. The successful reality star must be particularly attuned to the cues given off by the bachelor or bachelorette. When two people meet—particularly for the first time—multiple body language signals are emitted and received at various proximities. As your quarry approaches, read the following signals to know where you really stand in his or her heart. Body-language expert Patti Wood explains that while some nonverbal cues may be delivered consciously, no one can ever be in complete control of the physical cues they give off unconsciously. The eyes may be the window to the soul, but body language is the doorway to next week's solo date competition.

1) **Eyebrow flash.**

Occurs: 7 to 8 feet (2 to 2½ m) away

Description: The eyebrow flash is a gesture whereby the eyebrows raise and the eyes are opened a bit wider for a fraction of a second. Generally, this cue occurs when two people approach one another or when one person observes another coming toward her. It is a basic reflex where an individual instinctually recognizes "there's another person."

The Read: The eyebrow flash will tell you what is important to the other person. Notice where your bachelor or bachelorette looks directly after raising his or her eyebrows. If she looks down at herself, then she is self-conscious (due to the camera, your presence, or perhaps her own issues). If she looks at you, then she is interested in you and more at ease with herself.

((((INSIDER TIP))))

When two people appear to the audience to meet for the first time on a reality show, this "first time" may actually occur two or three times. Often, a first meeting or entrance will be reshot because a camera or microphone wasn't in the right place. You must pay close attention during your first meeting, as this will be your most honest read of your potential partner's body language. Pay attention to any retake reads to check for consistency.

2) **Smile.**

Occurs: 6 to 7 feet (1½ to 2 m) away

Description: Although the smile is one of the easiest cues to feign, it still effectively conveys to the receiver that there is nothing to fear.

The Read: Reading a smile correctly will help you determine how open and comfortable someone is with you. Particularly in the case of men (who stop giving frequent full-teeth smiles at about the age of six) but also in the case of women, a wide showing of the teeth with the corners of the mouth turned up indicates a great deal of comfort. A restricted, closed-mouth smile suggests that a person is not ready to expose everything. Pay careful attention to the first smile you receive from a bachelor or bachelorette and compare it to smiles you receive after you know each other better to determine whether he or she is opening up to you or shutting down.

Check the position of the heart to determine true feelings.

3) **Heart position.**

Occurs: 3 to 5 feet (1 to 1½ m) away

Description: This signal is simply the direction a bachelor or bachelorette's upper chest faces, and is therefore the direction of his or her heart. The feet may point one direction and the head may point another, but the position of the heart indicates what is most important to a bachelor or bachelorette.

The Read: If a person's heart is facing toward you, then he or she is open to you and feels comfortable exposing his or her emotional state to you. If a bachelor or bachelorette's heart faces a camera, then you may assume that the camera is most important and you may question his or her motives. Use this signal both initially and in further rounds to note which potential suitors a bachelor or bachelorette's heart prefers.

4) **The embrace.**

Occurs: Up to 2 feet (½ m) away

Description: The position and action of the hands during an embrace will give you a closer look at a bachelor or bachelorette's true motivation.

The Read: When interpreting hand cues during a hug, you must take into account the signals that came before it. Does it feel natural and consistent with the cue that came before the touch? Additionally, note the specific position of the hands on your body during the hug. If they are closer to more sensual areas (neck, waist, behind), then your quarry is exhibiting sexual attraction to you. Conversely,

BODY LANGUAGE CUES BY GENDER

Use these gender-specific signals to help guide your strategy and tailor your expectations of the bachelor or bachelorette. If you are receiving all the right signals, keep doing what you are doing. If you are receiving some questionable signals, rethink your strategy.

Men

* Men who are sexually attracted to you will sit with their legs open (as opposed to crossed, showing the sole of a foot, which may indicate a desire for dominance or a closed emotional attitude).

* Where the feet go, the heart follows. In a group setting, the direction a man's feet point will indicate his focus. If they are pointed to you, then he is interested in you. If they point away from you or toward other men, then he is interested in defending himself against the group.

Women

* When lined up, women will touch their hair, jewelry, or face in a nonverbal attempt at attracting attention. Women may touch a necklace or an earring to draw attention to a specific part of their body. A quick earring grab may indicate nervousness. A slow and alluring necklace grab may indicate availability. Touching the hair or face may be an attempt to show off their beauty.

* Women who are sexually attracted to you will cross their legs in your direction, with the upper leg toward you. Conversely, this action also closes off men on the opposite side of the leg cross.

touching areas such as the arms, shoulders, and the middle of the back indicates a more reluctant attraction.

((((INSIDER TIP))))

Place the most trust in your impressions of body language during shot set-ups or when the cameras stop rolling for tape changes, lighting adjustments, or other technical operations. At these "down times," the pressure is off, and everyone in the cast and crew relaxes a bit. These moments of unaffected behavior will give you the clearest indications of others' reactions to you.

HOW TO MAKE THE MOST OF YOUR DATE

The most difficult part of dating on a reality show is that you will likely have only one chance to convince your date that you are exactly who she is looking for. When you have the opportunity to be alone with a potential love interest, you must stand out from your competitors. If you choose to be yourself, then you are putting your faith in the hands of fate—if you are meant to be together, you are meant to be together—and there is little advice that can be offered to help keep you in the game. But if you want to boost your chances, dating advisor Eve Hogan and psychologist Dr. Barry Goldstein recommend employing the following techniques to convince your date that you're the One.

1) **Make eye contact.**

Hold eye contact a bit longer than is comfortable—but do not stare.

2) **Create similar interests.**

Ask your date what his favorites are (food, colors, places to visit) and then say, "Mine too."

3) **Attempt to finish your date's sentences.**

Listen to your date closely as he describes something close to his heart (a belief, adage, or other value-based statement). You should be able to recognize one or two words just as he begins to say them. Say these words with him, simultaneously.

If your date isn't responding to your advances, you may need
to play the producers to increase your time on the show.

4)   Laugh and touch your date simultaneously.

As you enjoy your date's wit and humor, reach out and touch him in a suggestive but nonthreatening location (arms, thighs, abdomen).

5)   Be appreciative of your date.

Thank him for joining you for the evening and mention that you feel you have made a "connection."

((((INSIDER TIP))))

Due to the logistics of clearing locations, obtaining permits, and all the other technical issues involved in television, you may not have control over where you go for your date. You will have to impress your date in whatever environment the producers choose and under whatever circumstances they throw your way.

How to Play for Time

If your date falls apart, your best bet for staying on the show is to solicit help from the producers to ensure that you are passed over in the next elimination round. A bachelor or bachelorette usually has one or two definite front-runners in mind, but can be undecided on whom else to keep around. A subtle suggestion from a trusted producer often tips the balance for a contestant who is "on the bubble." Convince the producer to do her best to keep you around by becoming her casting dream. Use any of the following strategies to secure your place for at least another week.

1) **Pick a fight with one of your top competitors.**

Comment on the way he dresses, how he chews his food, or how he woke you up when he came into your room drunk at 3 A.M. Argue loudly and irrationally, but *do not* make physical contact. Continue your days on the show in constant conflict with this person.

2) **Announce a devious strategy in a private interview with the producers, and work to pull it off.**

If one of your competitors has a date that evening, volunteer to make lunch and then go overboard on the garlic to sabotage his chances for an intimate moment.

3) **Create and become an outlandish character.**

Claim that you are using mind-control techniques to win over your date, but make that assertion in the privacy of your room or in a confessional interview so that your outrageous plan will be hidden from your love interest. Or cry early and often during interviews with the producer.

4) **Declare yourself the underdog early in the show.**

By telling your competitors and the producer that you have no chance of winning, every elimination round you survive will serve as a small victory for the "little guy." Audiences (and in turn producers) love to see such bootstrap victory stories.

HOW TO DISCERN WHETHER YOUR DATE IS ACTUALLY WEALTHY

Reality relationship shows have undertaken a series of experiments to determine the true nature of love. Some of these programs attempt to determine how important wealth is when considering a potential mate. If you plan on participating in any relationship show, you must learn how to determine whether you are facing a Vanderbilt heir or a Peterbilt driver. Whether you are digging for gold or unearthing a fraud, dating expert Patti Stanger offers the following truths.

1)   **The wealthy get good tickets.**

As a general rule, the wealthy receive the very best seats at major events. A genuinely wealthy man will have no difficulty sharing stories about his experiences at the World Series or Super Bowl and his opera-box view of Pavarotti's performance at the Kennedy Center.

The Test: Determine his favorite sports team and then ask him to tell you about the last time he went to a game.

Failing Grade: He admits, "They always sell out. I can't get tickets."

Passing Grade: He regales you with a story involving rubbing shoulders with celebrities who shared his VIP seating.

Extra Points: He tells you his family owns a major sports team.

2)   **The wealthy are well educated.**

Almost anyone born of wealth will have attended a prestigious boarding school or university, if only for several semesters. It is the very rare millionaire who went to a community college or skipped school altogether.

The Test: Ask your potential millionaire, "So, where did you go to school?"

Failing Grade: He tells you the name of his public high school.

Passing Grade: He names a university you've heard of.

Extra Points: He talks about his graduate degree from an Ivy League business school.

digital watch

bad table manners

used napkin on table

Observe your date closely to determine wealth and breeding.

3) **The wealthy have traveled.**

Most people who've grown up with money have been overseas several times and have seen the world. They also have knowledge of the amenities of first-class travel and know something about private jets.

The Test: Mention your desire to travel to Milan, Barcelona, Hong Kong, Paris, or the French Riviera.

Failing Grade: He claims that he's more of a homebody, and even when he has to travel he likes to stay in.

Passing Grade: He provides an informed discussion of his favorite activities, restaurants, and "unknown" jazz clubs in an exotic foreign city or other destination.

Extra Points: He one-ups your story about upgrading on American Airlines with an amusing Gulfstream V anecdote.

4) **The wealthy have manners.**

Almost all well-bred wealthy men are schooled in etiquette. They will open doors, slide in your chair, or offer an arm when climbing stairs. The wealthy also know wines and rarely take a first sip without raising their glass to you with a very short toast.

The Test: Observe his actions as he takes a seat at the dinner table.

Failing Grade: He studies the utensils, clearly trying to remember the tips he's been given about which fork to use first.

Passing Grade: He automatically places his napkin on his lap.

Extra Points: When your food arrives, he waits as you take your first bite. He does not touch his plate with his utensil before you do.

5)   **The wealthy have nice watches.**

People rarely wear their own clothes on a reality show, so the way your potential millionaire is dressed will not disclose much. However, almost all wealthy men wear nice watches, and if he's the real deal he will most likely insist on wearing his own.

The Test: Ask for the time, then comment on the man's wristwatch.

Failing Grade: He says he prefers digital to analog watches.

Passing Grade: He will be able to tell you more about the watch than you care to hear, including a story involving his father.

Extra Points: Your comment leads to a discussion of his collection of antique self-winding chronographs.

6)   **The wealthy never talk about their money.**

The *nouveau riche* may hint at roughly how many stock options they cashed out at the height of the internet bubble, but "old money" never reveals anything specific about their wealth. Ever.

The Test: Ask him point blank how much he's worth.

Failing Grade: He answers with a specific amount, or even hints at a real number.

Passing Grade: He admits, "I wouldn't know. Most of our holdings are in a blind trust."

Extra Points: He says, "Enough to be happy, because happiness comes from being able to support so many good causes."

HOW TO SPOT A PLOT TWIST

The "twist" has become a crucial lynchpin of the reality show, and home audiences can't get enough of them. Today's reality stars need to have finely tuned antennas, and while it's impossible to stay one step ahead of the producers all the time, it is in your best interest to be suspicious of every aspect of the show. Here is a list of questions that should constantly swirl through your mind as you participate.

*   Does the overall premise of the show seem sound? A thin premise can be either the result of shoddy development or an intentional feint to disguise the true nature of the show.

*   Have you been briefed on the entire arc of the show, including the ending? If you are not completely clear on how the series will end, a twist may be coming.

*   Does the premise seem similar to a show that has already aired? If you have been cast in a show that seems to be an exact copy of a hit show, assume that a twist will arise to differentiate your show from the previous version.

*   Did one of your fellow contestants suddenly change course and do something unexpected? This might be a sign that the contestant is a plant or has been coerced by the producers.

*   Have you been approached by the producers with a side deal? If the producers offer you a secret exemption or immunity, assume they've made the offer to others.

HOW TO ESCAPE THE MICROPHONES

Everyone has secrets. Everyone, that is, but the stars of a reality-television show. With microphones recording everything you say, there is no place to hide. Sometimes, however, you may need to have a quiet word with someone—out of range of the microphones. Perhaps you and another contestant need to exchange ideas without the producers knowing what you are doing, or perhaps you want to profess your feelings to someone without the whole country knowing the full story. Is there any way to escape the prying ears of the microphones? There is, if you follow this advice reluctantly suggested by ace audio mixer Stacy Hill.

1) **Get wet.**

Remove your lav mic and jump into the pool or ocean. The maneuver will cause the audio department to scramble to record you with a boom mic. As long as you stay in the middle of the pool or away from shore and splash the water as you speak, you will be able to speak your mind without being recorded.

((((INSIDER TIP))))

Having a conversation near a running sink or shower may make the audio quality subpar to broadcast standards, but your words will still be discernable and could be subtitled on the screen.

Jumping in water without your mic may allow you to have a brief private conversation.

2) Play music.

Have private conversations while copyrighted music is playing loudly. The music will distort the audio of your voice, and the show's producers will not want to go to the expense of clearing the rights to broadcast the song playing in the background. Situations like this will be rare, because reality-show environments are kept music-free for just these reasons. In extreme cases, you can ask a friend to loudly sing a popular song while you quickly convey information.

3) Remove the microphone's battery.

Turning off your body mic is an easy way to stop recording, but the audio department will be able to tell that it is no longer transmitting and will immediately fix the problem. If you truly want to foil them, remove the battery from the bottom of the transmitter and throw it away. The audio technicians will never suspect and will troubleshoot for several minutes until they finally discover the missing battery. This is a subterfuge that can only be used once. Be aware that your conversation partner's microphone continues to record everything you say unless you take steps to disable it as well.

4) **Put the microphone in your pocket.**

Your body mic is most likely clipped to your shirt front. While nobody is looking, move the microphone to your rear pocket. The audio technician will still be getting a signal from your transmitter, but he will not hear your whispers. Make sure not to overuse this technique—you don't want your trick to be discovered.

5) **Use inappropriate language.**

If all else fails, use blue language that could never be broadcast on television. The producers will be able to hear and understand what you are saying, but they will not be able to use the conversation on the show. You must use obscenities to replace almost all of the verbs and nouns in your sentences so that even if your conversation is "bleeped," nobody will be able to understand completely what you are saying. Then again, your castmate may not understand what you are trying to say, either.

Microphones 101

Wireless Body Lav Mic

What it is: A small, lightweight microphone designed to record the audio of the person wearing it. It consists of two parts, connected by a wire: the microphone (the size of a pencil eraser) and the transmitter (the size of a deck of cards).

Location: The microphone is worn on the body, clipped to a shirt, or in the hair. The transmitter is placed in a rear pocket or strapped to the small of the back.

Range: Can record a whisper at about 3 feet (1 m).

Boom Mic

What it is: A microphone affixed to a long pole, allowing the audio assistant to move it just out of camera shot. Sometimes used as the primary microphone, sometimes used to back up the body mics. This microphone is often protected by a wind-guard.

Location: Held by an audio assistant.

Range: Can record a whisper at up to 15 feet (4½ m).

Parabolic Mic

What it is: A directional microphone (meaning that it needs to be aimed at the audio source) that can record distant sounds. Only rarely used on reality shows, these microphones can often be seen at sporting events. The microphone sits inside a large dish.

Location: Usually hidden from sight.

Range: Can record a whisper up to 150 feet (46 m).

HOW TO HOOK UP ON CAMERA

Is there anything better than the moment when love blossoms on a reality show? It creates a great story: Boy meets girl (or girl meets boy, or boy meets boy) in the most unlikely of circumstances, and against all odds they fall in love. Networks and producers get very excited when their cast members fall in love, especially on shows that aren't geared toward matchmaking. But as attraction turns to passion, what is the randy reality star to do? If you find that your libido is trumping your mental resources, several producers (who choose to remain nameless) offer the following pointers.

1) **Be prepared.**

Make sure that everything you need to complete your task is waiting under the covers. Running from the bed to retrieve a crucial item from a suitcase or the bathroom will give the producers the perfect chance to show all the world just what you are up to.

2) **Remain aware of the cameras.**

Even if you manage to remove yourself from the presence of the film crew, you can be sure that you are still being recorded. Darkness provides false security, as cameras equipped with night vision can record without any visible light at all. Outside at night, cameras are much tougher to spot, and with long telephoto lenses you can be photographed from several hundred feet away. See "Finding the Hidden Cameras" on page 96 for some common hiding places.

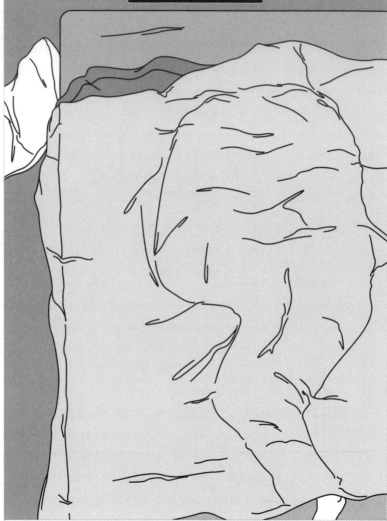

Cover yourselves entirely with a blanket, keep noise to a minimum, and remain aware of the cameras at all times.

3) **Keep noise to a minimum.**

Even if you've stripped yourselves of your body mics, there is still a chance that a hidden directional microphone is aimed at the two of you, capturing every sound. Be as quiet as possible.

((((INSIDER TIP))))

When you are alone with a potential love interest in any location (in a room, on a beach, or in the woods), know that there is a good chance the material will be edited, scored, and even subtitled to suggest that you are more intimately involved than may actually be the case. If chastity is a foundation of your character, avoid playful one-on-one encounters entirely, especially late at night.

4) **Avoid pillow talk.**

Although most networks are not able to use the audio or video of a couple in the act, the conversation afterward can lead an audience to draw an obvious conclusion. You can cuddle, but quietly, without talking.

5) **Keep your business to yourself the next day.**

Your hook-up may change an aspect of your strategy or create complications for you with the other contestants or back at home (in the "real" real world). When confronted by any roommates, competitors, or others, you and your partner should keep the events of the night before to yourselves.

FINDING THE HIDDEN CAMERAS

You'd be surprised at how "obvious" hidden cameras are. Cameras can be as small as a cigarette, and they can be concealed almost anywhere. Here are some popular hidden reality-show cameras:

* The briefcase cam.

    A briefcase left on the nightstand may very well house a recording device.

* One-way-mirror cam.

    Mirrors and smoked glass are perfect disguises for cameras. Assume that there is a camera behind every mirror in the house, including your bedroom and the bathroom.

* Secret agent cam.

    Clocks, false paintings, microwave ovens, VCR displays, lampshades, television screens, heating ducts, foliage, stereo faceplates, thick eyeglasses, and architectural details can all house a small secret camera.

HOW TO ENDEAR YOURSELF TO THE PARENTS

Charming the parents of a potential date or spouse on a reality show is extremely stressful. A mouth free of gum and a scent free of smoke, alcohol, or overbearing cologne is only half the battle. Once you have found your way into the parents' home, your most difficult task will be finding your way into their hearts. Relationship advisor Eve Hogan explains that your only job when spending an evening or a weekend with the parents is to demonstrate that you are worthy of their (and their offspring's) affection.

1)   **Mirror the manner of the parents.**

People like people who are like them. If the parents are conservative, pull in your reins. If they are quiet, lower your voice. Additionally, psychological research indicates that a child's romantic relationships are generally modeled after parental relationships. Mirroring the behavior of the parents may have the extra benefit of subconsciously attracting your love interest to you—an element that is vital to parental approval.

2)   **Allow the parents to lead the conversation.**

If they are not open to easy conversation, you will need to take the lead, but be careful not to talk so much that no one else gets a word in edgewise. However, avoid discussing politics and religion. If these subjects are broached, make a quick noncommittal statement and change the subject.

DO

Compliment home décor.

DON'T

Help around the house, but don't overdo it.

3)   **If the parents do not take the lead in the conversation, select an object in the home and offer a compliment about it.**

People surround themselves with symbols that reveal what is important to them. Notice the theme of the home—spiritual, athletic, artistic, worldly—and allow their trappings to inspire a question. If there are trophies, ask about the sport or event for which they were received. If there is artwork, ask about a piece that speaks to you.

4)   **Make eye contact whenever you speak.**

Eye contact is an important indicator of honesty. Focus the majority of your attention on the person with whom you are speaking, while connecting briefly with others in the room. Do not overdo the eye contact with your love interest when you're in the presence of the parents.

5)   **Help around the house.**

Offer to help with the cooking and the dishes. If you are spending an evening or two in the home, make your bed immediately after waking up. If the father is working on a project on the house or yard, offer a hand. Surprising the parents by preparing breakfast or mowing the lawn is overdoing it.

6)   **Be gracious and informative when you leave.**

Thank the parents for their hospitality, and let them know how much you enjoyed meeting them. Assure them that both the emotional and physical safety of their son or daughter is your number one priority.

HOW TO DATE MULTIPLE PARTNERS

As the star of a relationship reality show with only nine episodes to decide who your soulmate will be, you must become a dating multitasker. You will be in dozens of relationships simultaneously, and while that certainly has a hedonistic upside (who hasn't dreamed of dating dozens of perfect specimens?), it also has a serious downside on a reputation level (since most of the viewing audience will express their secret jealousy of you through moral outrage). Add to this the conflicted emotions of being torn between 25 lovers and an ever-increasing count of ousted dates, and you have one harried bachelor or bachelorette. Producer Kathy Wetherell presents the following suggestions for becoming a Teflon Casanova.

1)   **Live completely in the present.**

The only way to get through multiple dates in one weekend is to stay entirely focused on the present. Thinking about your previous partner or anticipating the next one will throw you off your game. Focus anew as soon as each date starts. Do not allow anything to distract you from complimenting, listening to, and extending your now-famous charm to the potential mate you are with.

2)   **Freshen up between dates.**

Use soap and water to eliminate or minimize any residual cologne, perfume, or lipstick from your previous date. This action will also give you a fresh start on your next date.

DATING MULTIPLE PARTNERS

Strive for the same level of intimacy with each date.

3) Remember that when you date one, you date them all.

If all of the contestants are housed together, they will compare notes. Everything you do with one will be considered by all, so a serious gaffe with one date represents a serious gaffe with all of the housemates.

4) Treat each potential mate differently.

If your date with the first finalist goes very well, you will be tempted to use the same techniques with the next date. Do not. The audience won't forgive you, and once the finalists compare notes, they won't forgive you, either.

5) Strive for the same level of intimacy with each date.

If one date session ends with a quick peck in the hotel lobby while another ends in deep carnal understanding, you may end up with a political mess that will take several episodes to sort out.

HOW TO OFFER A NONBINDING PROPOSAL

If you are unsure that the last contestant standing is indeed your new life partner, you'll need to strike a balance between fulfilling your obligations to your mate, yourself, and the viewing audience. Relationship advisor and family lawyer Sherry Zimmerman recommends proposing in a way that saves face, saves emotions, and, effectively, saves ratings.

Conditional Proposal

Adapt the following language to suit your circumstance:

"We've built a great connection to each other in such a short amount of time, and you are someone I can see myself sharing my life with. If we had more time, I would wait until we'd been dating several more months, and if things kept moving in the right direction I'd propose to you. I'm as nervous about jumping the gun as you are, but I would rather take a chance proposing than take a chance on losing out on the great future we could have together. Will you say yes to marrying me, and promise me that we will spend the next six months building on what we've started and then set a wedding date?"

Conditional Acceptance

When accepting a proposal on reality television, leave yourself the same loopholes recommended for proposals. Adjust the language below to your circumstance:

"I feel the same way about you, in principle. And, yes, I will say yes to marrying you and then build on what we have begun. As long as our goals, values, and attraction continue to grow as they have over the last few weeks, we can then set a wedding date."

CHAPTER 4

SURVIVAL SKILLS

One thing is certain on a survival-based reality show—you must be able to pull your survival weight. Being a brilliant outdoorsman isn't enough to ensure your victory in and of itself, but knowing how to build a fire, locate and purify water (let alone get it back to your camp), and build a shelter will provide you with an advantage over your less-resourceful competitors. A bit of pre-show know-how will give you what you need to make the essentials easier to secure.

Once you've set up camp, food will be a valuable commodity, and if you can provide it for your team, you'll become indispensible. If catching the day's protein ration is not enough, then a little survival cooking could be just the trick, since the way to your teammates' good graces is through their stomachs. Staying alive—whether by procuring food, surviving wildlife encounters, or enduring the tribe's votes against you—is vital to your post-reality career. A little in-field medical training may also be just the thing you need to keep your head off the chopping block.

In this chapter you'll learn all you need to thrive in the survival game.

HOW TO MAKE FIRE

Fire should be your first goal when you get to camp on a survival show. You will use fire to cook, stay warm, purify water, and provide light for late-night conversation. Building a successful fire is your best opportunity to build early team respect. Here's how, according to survival expert Mel Deweese.

1) **Choose a location for your fire.**

Select an area that is away from the elements (i.e., tides or heavy winds), but clear enough for you to be able to build a shelter around the fire once it is established (see step 6).

2) **Gather materials.**

Collect both small and large pieces of wood, dry twigs, brush, leaves, and tree sap.

3) **Prepare your pit and kindling.**

Dig a narrow pit about 6 to 10 inches (15 to 25 cm) deep and 2 to 3 feet (60 to 90 cm) in circumference and arrange dry twigs, brush, or leaves in a small pile. Use tree sap or your own earwax spread over your kindling as lubricant.

4) **Focus a pinpoint of sunlight on your kindling with a lens.**

Use a bifocal or farsighted prescription eyeglass lens, flashlight lens, or a magnifying glass to focus a beam of sunlight on the kindling to start the fire. Blow lightly on the smoke to create a flame.

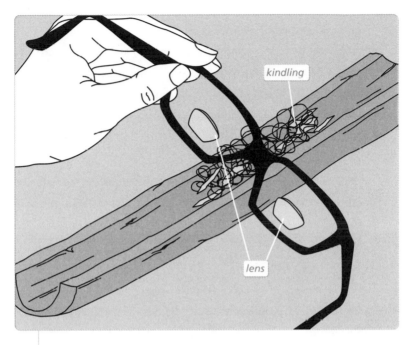

kindling

lens

5) **Fuel your fire with larger pieces of wood.**

Add more small twigs and brush to build the flames. Do not smother the fire by putting too much fuel on it—as your flames grow, stack larger pieces of wood in the shape of a pyramid so as not to snuff out any building flames.

((((INSIDER TIP))))

Firestarting should be a team effort—do not act as the leader. A first-day alpha dog is sure to be eliminated early. You want to be the hero—and be the one who actually starts the fire—but you don't want to stand out. Accept and make suggestions humbly.

6)   **Build a shelter for your fire.**

As soon as the fire is going strong, surround and cover the fire pit's area with live branches and leaves to protect it from the weather. Keep at least 4 feet (120 cm) of clearance on three sides and the top. Leave one side open to allow oxygen in.

7)   **Create an "active" fire.**

Once your original fire has developed coals, build a separate fire outside of the shelter to serve as your active fire. Maintain the original fire to keep the coals going, taking coals from it as needed to build new, smaller fires for cooking, boiling water, and warmth.

((((INSIDER TIP))))

If you fail to start a fire, rest assured that the show's production will provide you with the ability to make it. Producers would never actually let a team go for long without the ability to cook or make potable water. You may suffer a day or two, though, because a group without fire makes for entertaining television.

HOW TO MAKE A WATER PIPELINE

Depending on your location, you and your team will likely have to hike to get drinking water. Obtaining water and carrying it back to camp can be a time-consuming and exhausting task. If your camp is endowed with plentiful bamboo and is situated downhill from your water source, a water pipeline will save your team a tremendous amount of time and energy. Be the one to spearhead this project, and your teammates are not likely to eliminate you soon. Survivalist Mel Deweese lays out the following steps.

1) **Determine the distance from your camp to the water source.**
Count your strides as you hike to the source, and then check your count as you return.

2) **Chop down several bamboo stalks to use as piping.**
Cut and lay out numerous long sections of bamboo about 2 inches (5 cm) in diameter. Lay them end to end on the ground, and count your strides as you walk alongside them. Be sure the length of the combined bamboo matches the stride distance to the water source.

3) **Hollow out the bamboo.**
Using a narrower piece of bamboo at least half as long, hollow out each of the long pieces you've cut.

4)   Wash each hollowed-out bamboo piece in the river or ocean. Scrub the bamboo thoroughly with a leaf. Clean any white powder off both the bamboo and your skin to avoid irritation.

5)   Lay the pipe.
Starting at your water source or as close as you can manage, lay the sections of bamboo on a downhill slope toward your camp. Temporarily secure each section in place with several rocks.

DRINKING WATER BASICS

At your remote location, water must be boiled to eliminate bacteria and make it drinkable. Use the following rules of thumb:

* At sea level, boil water for 3 minutes.
* For every 1,000 feet (300 m) above sea level, boil water for an additional minute.
* Save and use all potable water for drinking and cooking. Do not wash your underwear or yourself in potable water, or you'll risk the ire of your teammates and competitors.

6)   Make connection pieces out of bamboo.
Cut as many connector pieces as are needed, each about 6 inches (15 cm) long and twice the width of the pipeline. Use the bamboo pipes of the pipeline to hollow out just enough of the center of the connectors to ensure a snug fit. Clean the connectors out thoroughly. Connect two sections of pipe by pressing each halfway into the connector.

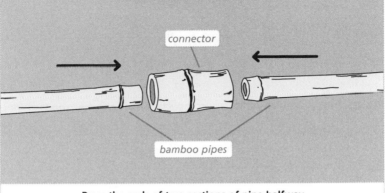

CONNECTING THE PIPELINE

connector

bamboo pipes

**Press the ends of two sections of pipe halfway
into the connecting piece.**

7)   **Cap the camp-side end of your pipeline.**

Insert a rock, a piece of wood, or a section of unhollowed bamboo that is nearly the same size as the opening at the end of your pipeline to help control the flow of water.

8)   **Start the flow of water.**

When your camp needs more fresh water, only one or two people need to walk out to the source—and no one will have to carry a heavy load back to camp. Place the feed end of your pipeline in the water to send it down toward your camp. If your water source is a well, fill a bucket and pour water into the pipeline to get it moving. Make a funnel out of a strong leaf to lead the water into the pipe.

HOW TO BUILD SHELTER

Shelter is fourth on the list of vital necessities on a survival-based reality show. Fire, water, and alliances come first—although building shelter and building alliances (see "How to Form an Alliance" on page 40) often go hand in hand. Your shelter (like your alliance) will provide you with protection and security. Survival expert Mel Deweese explains that your shelter must be well located, well built, and well maintained.

1) **Choose a safe and secure shelter location.**

Select a spot that is:

- Free of insects, rodent or snake burrows, and poisonous plants.
- Close to a plentiful supply of firewood.
- Not threatened by leaning or dying trees, which could fall on your shelter during a storm.
- Out of a flood zone. Check the landscape around and upstream from your potential shelter locale. Assess the natural flow of water in the landscape, and select a spot that is clear of the floodplain.

((((INSIDER TIP))))

Construct your shelter so that it opens to the west. You will increase your on-camera time by providing camera crews with a perfect shot of the sleeping team as the sun rises, a time of day known throughout the entertainment industry as the "magic hour" because of the diffuse and rosy light.

2)   Gather materials.

Collect enough wood (bamboo or other hardwood) to form a base and a lean-to roof. The wood for the roof should be about 2 feet (60 cm) longer than the wood for the foundation. Collect several 2- to 3-foot (60 to 90 cm) lengths of wide wood—preferably with a forked top end—for your foundation. Also gather rattan vine or thin riverbank roots to use as rope to tie the shelter together, and numerous palm leaves or other heavy, broad vegetation for thatching.

3)   Build the foundation.

Pound or press the short sections of wood into solid ground at each corner of your shelter. Be sure that at least 1 to 2 feet (30 to 60 cm) of the wood remain above ground. Using an "X" pattern with your rope, tie a frame around the shorter sections of wood. Keep your foundation off the ground by at least a few inches. While this will not guarantee that you will avoid scorpions, snakes, insects, and other pests, it will minimize your chances of contact. Tie several crossbeam joists running east to west between the frame, and then tie the floor onto the joists running north to south.

4)   Frame the roof.

Frame a roof using the same technique explained in step 3. Your roof should be 2 feet (30 cm) wider than your foundation, and will provide a secure overhang for the sides of the shelter. Tie one crossbeam every 2 feet running east to west and then north to south to form a series of grids.

((((INSIDER TIP))))

Upon your arrival on a survival show, you may find that the location of your camp has been preselected. Preselection is done so that producers and crews have as much control as possible—the camp's location will determine what backgrounds will be seen behind you during confessional interviews, how far the crew will be from your camp, the quality of the light, available amenities, and more. Additionally, your campsite will already be lit, wired, and outfitted with microphones before you arrive. You will have to pick the exact spot for your shelter within the parameters of the existing site.

5) **Shingle your roof.**

Start at the top of your roof frame and lay on the palm leaves. As you work your way down, lay the leaves under the edge of the leaves above, as roofing shingles are laid. Tie each row to the frame in turn.

6) **Lean the roof up and secure it to nearby trees or support posts.**

7) **Maintain the shelter.**

Continue to work on your shelter every day, even after you think it is complete. Strengthen any joints or joists tied together with rope or vine. Add large leaves to your roof to thicken the protective layering. The work you do daily may not seem necessary, but it is sure to help the shelter stay intact in case there is a large storm.

REALITY SHOW SHELTER

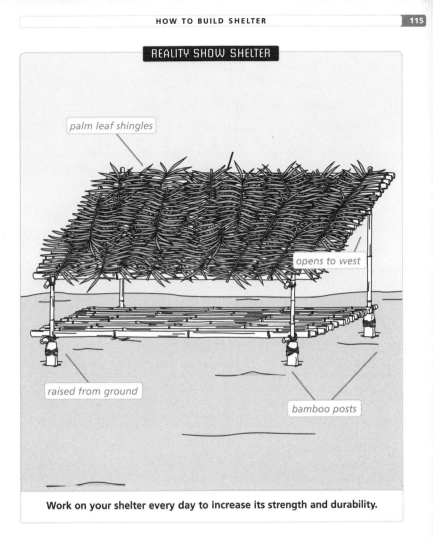

palm leaf shingles

opens to west

raised from ground

bamboo posts

Work on your shelter every day to increase its strength and durability.

PERSONAL ITEMS FOR REALITY CONDITIONS

Some reality shows allow contestants to bring along a personal item. While many contestants choose items with religious or emotional value, you might want to consider one of the following practical choices:

* **Moist towelettes,** with antibacterial solution for cleaning your hands, face, and body.

* **Baking soda,** which has hundreds of uses: soap, toothpaste, deodorant, clothing detergent, bee-sting poultice, dish cleanser, odor reducer, and more. It can even make beans more digestible.

* **Salt** can be a seasoning, dentifrice, mouthwash, pot cleaner, ant repellent, and more.

* **Fishing line,** which can be used to hang objects, join items for construction projects, and trap fish.

* **Compact multiuse tool,** such as a pocketknife, which will come in handy when cutting vines, cleaning fish or other food, and many other situations.

* **Straight edge razor,** which can be used for shaving and basic cutting tasks.

HOW TO CATCH FOOD

Although you will never be left to starve on a survival reality show, you will get just enough food to keep you alive—approximately 600 calories a day. Your best bet for survival—physically, mentally, and competitively— is to take the food situation into your own hands; no one wants to eliminate the one bringing in meat. Survival expert Mel Deweese offers a quick lesson in Neanderthal reality.

Small Wildlife

Use the following technique to land yourself a rodent, squirrel, or even a boar.

1) Make a rope.

Gather several vines or thin tree roots (these are easiest to procure from a soft riverbank) at least 4 feet (120 cm) long. Strip at least three thin pieces from the vine or root, tie the pieces together at one end, and braid them tightly. This will increase the strength of your rope. In order for your trap to be most effective, make the rope at least 3 feet (91 cm) long.

2) Scout for good hunting ground.

Walk through dense forest, fields of tall grass, or along the water. Look for trampled areas covered with droppings or hair—signs that animals may frequent the area.

PLAN AHEAD

With some forethought—and a willingness to bend the rules—you can sneak sections of strong, synthetic rope onto the show. You will need two 2-foot-long (60 cm) pieces of parachute cord (a strong, flexible, and broad string used in parachuting); and two 4-foot-long (120 cm) pieces of 550 cord (a thin, very strong military cord made of braided nylon and protected by a nylon sheath). Both cords are available at military surplus or climbing stores.

1) Disassemble one of the parachute cords.

    Draw back about an inch of the parachute cord to reveal a thin wire. Pinch the wire and pull it out of the surrounding cord.

2) Insert the 550 cord into the parachute cord.

    Fold one piece of the 550 cord in half and tape the fold to the wire you removed from the parachute cord. Push the wire and 550 cord into the parachute cord until it comes out the other end. Remove the tape, and withdraw the wire.

3) Replace your shoelace with the doctored parachute cord.

4) Repeat steps 1 to 3 with the other parachute cord, and lace up your other shoe.

5) After arriving at the show's remote location, secretly unpack the 550 cord from your shoelaces.

6) Carry the cord into the ocean while swimming.

    As you emerge from the water, claim to have found the cord in the sea.

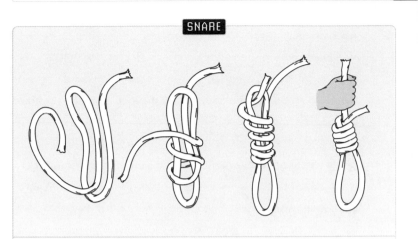

SNARE

Make a fist-sized noose to trap boars and large rodents.

3) Make a snare.

Observe the droppings to determine how large a snare to make. As a general rule, pea-sized droppings require a fist-sized snare and rice-sized droppings require a snare as wide as the circumference of two fingers. Form a loop at one end of the rope or cord to correspond with the size of the droppings. Tie the loop into a noose (see diagram above).

4) Lay the noose on the path of your potential catch.

Lay the noose flat on a narrow section of an already-trampled path. Animals generally will take the easiest path when walking through heavily forested areas or tallgrass fields.

5)   Anchor the snare to a tree or rock.

Tie square knots to secure the anchor to an immobile object. When an animal steps into the snare, one of its feet will naturally activate the noose action of your trap, closing the loop around its foot and trapping the animal.

6)   Leave the area, but return to check your snare frequently.

If you stay in the immediate area, your scent—which will likely be quite strong after several days on the show—will drive away potential meals. However, to avoid losing your food to another animal, return every hour or two to check your trap.

Fish

1)   Make a rope.

Gather several vines or thin tree roots (these are easiest to procure from a soft riverbank) at least 3 feet (90 cm) long. Strip at least three thin pieces from the vine or root, tie the pieces together at one end, and braid them tightly. This will increase the strength of your rope. Tie several pieces together to create a 3- to 4-foot (90 to 120 cm) section. Use a fisherman's knot to secure the rope (see diagram on page 121).

2)   Find a firm stick or branch with a forked end.

The branch should be strong enough to withstand the pull of a one-pound (.45 kg) fish but flexible enough to bend when your fish takes the bait. Willows or thin bamboo, if available, serve this purpose well.

3) | **Tie the rope or vine onto the branch.**

Tie the rope in a fisherman's knot (see diagram below) just below the forked end of the stick to keep the rope from slipping off. Test your pole by tugging firmly on the far end of the line.

4) | **Locate a small animal bone.**

Scour the area for a small bone, preferably a rib bone or wishbone.

5) | **Hone the bone into a hook.**

Scrape the bone on a sharp rock to sand one end into a sharp point. Notch the bone just below the point to form a barb, completing the hook.

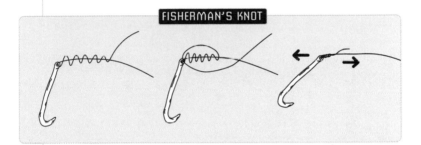

FISHERMAN'S KNOT

6) | **Tie the hook onto the loose end of the braided rope.**

Use a fisherman's knot (see diagram above) to secure the hook to the rope.

7) | **Gather bait.**

Look for worms, insects, or even smaller fish. Check under rocks near the riverbank to determine what types of insects or larvae might be consumed by the fish.

((((INSIDER TIP))))

If you are having trouble locating bait for your fishing expedition, seek out a small creek. Build a damn to divert the flow of water, then check in the original riverbed for minnows or other small river life that can be used as bait for larger fish.

8) **Bait the hook and drop it in the water.**

Drop your line near eddies or marshy banks in an ocean or river. As a general rule, the warmer the day, the deeper and more hidden the fish.

HOW TO COOK IN THE WILD

Being able to catch food for your team is an invaluable skill, but knowing how to cook your trappings into a palatable meal can keep you on the show indefinitely. A month of limited calories from the same foods gets monotonous and can affect the group's morale. Finding a way to spice up the lives of your teammates and competitors creates a positive perception of you and your value to the team. Here are some creative recipes from survival chef Mel Deweese.

Bamboo Rice

This recipe will show your competitors how creative your rice-cooking skills can be.

1 BAMBOO SHOOT, SEVERAL INCHES WIDE, ABOUT 1 FOOT (30 CM) IN LENGTH, CUT AT THE JOINTS

1 PART RICE

2 PARTS POTABLE WATER

1) Hollow out one end of the bamboo using a stick or a narrower piece of bamboo, leaving about 2 inches (5 cm) of pulp just above the bottom joint.

2) Clean the bamboo in water, rinsing until all the loose pieces of pulp and white powder are gone. Wash the white powder from your skin to avoid irritation.

3) Place the rice inside the bamboo tube.

4) Fill the tube with potable water. (See "Drinking Water Basics" on page 110.)

5) Set the tube upright on the fire, propped against other bamboo tubes. (As long as there is moisture in the tube, the bamboo will not burn.) Boil the water and rice until tender, approximately 20 minutes. Check the water level and add more if it looks too dry. When the rice is tender, remove the tube from the fire and eat.

((((INSIDER TIP))))

Never claim to be a cook or gourmet chef (someone will find a way to turn it against you)—prepare these meals as if you are making them up as you go along, thereby showcasing your ingenuity.

Boiled Fish in Broth

Rather than simply roasting fish on a fire, boil them for a more filling, protein-rich fish soup. This recipe also works with meat from game you capture (see "How to Catch Food," on page 117).

1 TO 6 FISH, GUTTED AND CLEANED

WATER

1) Place the fish in a pot of boiling water and boil until no longer translucent—about 10 minutes per inch (4 minutes per cm) thickness. Transfer the pot from the fire to the sand or the ground.

2) Use a spoon to remove the fish from the broth; cut each fish into equal pieces and distribute to the group. Serve with the broth and rice (see "Bamboo Rice" on page 123), if available.

Corn Cakes

For breakfast or a pre-challenge snack, corn cakes provide a tasty burst of energy (or at least fill an empty stomach).

2 PARTS CORNMEAL

1 PART WATER

1) Set a large, smooth, flat rock in the fire and let it heat up. Use another rock to grind the cornmeal into a powder in a pitted rock or bowl.

2) In another bowl or carved-out tree stump, mix the cornmeal and water until it forms a thick paste. Knead for about 5 minutes to work out any lumps. The dough will be very sticky.

3) Form the dough into a flat, round disk, and place it on the pre-heated rock. Allow it to cook several minutes until slightly browned. Cool and serve.

EDIBLE BERRIES

Use the following rules of thumb when searching for edible berries:

* Blue and black berries are generally edible.
* Red berries are sometimes edible. (Offer one to a competitor and observe the results to see if they are all right to eat.)
* Avoid green or white berries.
* Avoid leaves and plants with milky sap or a parsley-like top.

Sea Urchin Surprise

While you should not actively fish for sea urchins, if you happen to step on or get stung by one (see "How to Treat Minor Medical Conditions: Jellyfish Stings," on page 133), you might as well receive a meal for your pain.

1 FEMALE SEA URCHIN

POTABLE WATER

1) Poke the urchin with a sharp stick or machete to kill it. Carefully pry the urchin's shell apart using a knife or rock. Spilt the urchin down the center, avoiding its stingers.

2) Check to see if you have a female or male urchin. A male urchin is of little use to you, but a female urchin will have orange egg sacks at the bottom on either side.

3) Gently remove the egg sacks with a spoon or firm leaf and place them in a pan of cold, potable water. Swish the pan gently from side to side to clean the roe. Eat the eggs using your fingers or two thin but firm sticks as makeshift chopsticks.

THE 24-HOUR TASTE TEST

To determine whether indigenous plants are edible, use the following procedure.

1) Take a small (1/2 inch [1.5 cm]) piece of a plant common to your camp and put it in a pot of water.

2) Boil for 10 to 15 minutes. Remove and let cool.

3) Place the cooked piece of plant in your mouth. If there is no burning sensation, eat it.

4) Monitor your health for the next 8 hours. If there are no ill effects, boil several more pieces of plant and consume one every 8 hours for the next 16 hours.

5) If you don't become ill after a full day's experiment, you and your allies are safe to boil and consume the plant.

HOW TO DEAL WITH WILD ANIMALS

Wild landscapes provide the best storylines, as players accustomed to the city or suburbs come face to face with conditions and animals they would never encounter in their usual life. The locations chosen for reality shows are full of untamed animals that *will* come in contact with the players. Los Angeles Zoo curator Russ Smith suggests ways to stay safe.

Snakes

1) **Recognize a snake in a defensive posture.**

   A snake will coil, in whole or part, if it feels you are a threat to its safety or its ability to get where it wants to go. A snake that has drawn its head back or coiled its body is in a defensive posture and is ready to attack.

2) **Step or leap back at least a snake's length.**

   A snake can only lash out about a third of its length. Although most snakes can strike quickly, a step or leap to the side will give you time to clear its bite or give the snake the space it needs to make its escape.

3) **Back up and allow the snake to leave the area.**

   Once you are clear of the snake's striking distance, continue to back away from the area. Most snakes will leave without further incident.

If it is a small snake that refuses to leave, proceed to step 4. If a larger snake stays put, proceed to step 5.

4) Pick up a small snake with a strong stick and move it out of the area.

If you have no other choice but to move a small snake, look for a large stick with a forked end. Slide the stick under the snake about a third of the way down its body. Do not lift the snake by its tail. Lift the stick about 1 foot (30 cm) off the ground, then carefully and slowly carry it out of the way. Set the stick and the snake on the ground and back away.

5) Pick up a large snake with a strong stick and lower it into a bag or container.

Lift a large snake with a stick and transfer it to a bag or other lidded container. Carry the container away from the area and set it down gently. Open the container, back away, and allow the snake to exit.

Monkeys

Monkeys, particularly males, can be dangerous. A monkey that is used to eating in a particular area (such as your camp) may challenge you, with its teeth or claws, in a battle for food. Use the following strategy to avoid a monkey confrontation.

1) Store your food carefully and completely.

Monkeys are clever animals and can open closed containers. Put weights or heavy rocks on food containers to keep them upright and closed.

2)   **Dispose of food waste at least 2 miles (3.2 km) from your campground.**

Just because you're not interested in eating the waste doesn't mean that the monkeys won't be. Carry food waste far from camp to ensure that monkeys won't come looking for it.

3)   **Do not feed the monkeys.**

Offering food to a monkey will teach it that your camp is a viable food source. If you feed a monkey, he may return with other monkeys to look for food.

Throw a rock near the monkey to scare it away from the camp.

4) **If a monkey approaches your camp, throw a rock toward it.**
Do not try to hit the monkey, just aim to scare it away. After one or two incidents the monkey will learn to fear you, and you will only have to threaten to throw a rock at it.

5) **Do not grab food from a monkey.**
Once a monkey has stolen your food, let it go. Don't risk contracting disease or infection from a monkey bite.

Scorpions and Spiders

Scorpions and spiders are a common threat in many remote reality-show settings. These small creatures can easily slip past off-camera production defenses. Use the following techniques to avoid confrontation with scorpions or spiders.

1) **Shake out clothing, bedsheets, boots, and sleeping bags prior to use.**

2) **Do not walk barefoot.**

3) **Do not camp near or disturb small rock piles.**
Take extra precaution around any stacked woodpiles. These may house scorpions or spiders.

4) **Sleep in a shelter that is raised a few feet off the ground.**

5)   **Watch for spiders around the campfire.**

Light attracts moths and moths attract arachnids.

6)   **Be especially careful at night.**

The only way to avoid a scorpion or spider is to see it and veer off its path. Both creatures are primarily nocturnal, so keep your wits about you after the sun goes down.

((((INSIDER TIP))))

Reality shows that take place in rugged locations provide many layers of protection that are invisible to the cast. Highly trained specialists in heavy camouflage patrol the immediate area, usually equipped with rifles and nightvision goggles. Another security team patrols the outer perimeter. In addition, hidden security cameras are placed around the camps, both to track the movements of the contestants and to detect dangerous visitors. Snakes and other small predators are often allowed to enter camp, but only after the specialists deem them safe. Larger, more dangerous beasts are kept safely away.

HOW TO TREAT MINOR MEDICAL CONDITIONS

On a reality show, anything can happen. That's why production teams will always include at least one medic—if not an entire team—to deal with disasters. More serious injuries such as shark bites, severe burns, or broken bones will always be dealt with by skilled professionals. If, however, you or your reality mates suffer from jellyfish stings, minor burns, or diarrhea, chances are you'll be left to treat yourselves. Andrew Michaels, M.D., and Becky Fee, R.N., recommend the following skills for field triage and treatment to avoid infection and elimination.

Jellyfish Stings

1) **Remove the tentacles.**

To avoid a secondary sting, carefully lift the tentacles using any available material, including seaweed, clothing, a stick, or a seashell.

2) **Irrigate the wound.**

Use seawater or vinegar to flush out the wound. Do not use fresh water, alcohol, or urine to clean the area, as they may cause the nematocysts (stinging cells) to fire secondary venom.

3) **Neutralize the toxin.**

The best treatments for the toxin are unspiced meat tenderizer or a papaya paste—both of which contain the enzyme papain, which will break down the toxin's protein. Alternatively, apply baking soda, shaving cream, or mud to stabilize the nematocysts before proceeding to step 4.

4)　Remove damaged tissue retaining any nematocysts.

Carefully scrape away any damaged tissue using seawater and a sharpened seashell or knife. Be sure to sterilize your scraping instrument by boiling it in water for 5 minutes or holding it over a flame for 2 minutes (do not allow the knife blade to turn black).

5)　Reclean the wound.

Once all of the nematocysts and tentacles have been removed, clean the area with cooled but boiled drinking water. Sterilize a firm leaf or clean ribbon of clothing in boiling water and tie it over the wound. Check daily for infection.

Snakebites

If you or a teammate are bitten by a poisonous snake, a reality show's medical team will respond very quickly. Use the following techniques to assist them and limit the spread of venom.

1)　Take careful note of the snake.

Observe the snake's length, color, and other markings to help the show's medical team determine the correct antivenom. Do not attempt to capture the snake, or you may be bitten yourself.

2)   **Immobilize the victim.**

Lay the victim on the ground and be reassuring.

3)   **Isolate the bite area with two wide strips of clothing.**

Tear a T-shirt into strips and wrap one section above the bite area and one below to slow the spread of venom. Tie them snugly but not too tight—you must be able to feel a pulse. Check the wraps every few minutes and loosen them as swelling constricts the area.

MAKE YOUR OWN MEDICINE

If you find yourself hundreds of miles from a pharmacy and you've got the runs, you could be in trouble. Severe diarrhea can lead to dehydration, and dehydration leads to elimination from the game. The only sure-fire way to control your bowels when no other medication is available is to remove one piece of charcoal from the fire, allow it to cool, and grind it into a powder. Mix one palmful of powder into an 8-ounce (236-ml) cup of water and drink it down. Activated charcoal is used frequently in Western medicine to treat diarrhea, flatulence, and even poisoning. Although pure ground charcoal from your fire is not chemically processed as pharmaceutical charcoal is, it will still serve your survivalist purposes.

WILDERNESS HYGIENE TIPS

Several reality shows have challenged their casts to live without many of the luxuries we take for granted, including showers, baths, and washing machines. The small screen cannot convey how "ripe" reality contestants become after just a few days in camp—the heady aroma of body odor, sweaty clothing, and campfire smoke is overwhelming. We all know how important proper hygiene is, but what can be done to stay clean when living in the bush?

* **If you want to walk out a winner, take care of your feet.** In the wild, feet suffer the most from lack of hygiene, since they are a hotbed for bacteria and various "rots." Take off your shoes and air out your socks at least once every day. Allow both socks and shoes to dry completely before putting them back on. Massage bare feet to promote blood circulation.

* **Your personality should shine, not your skin.** Our bodies are used to being bathed most days a week, which means that oil rarely sits on our skin for long. In the wilderness, when that oil isn't removed, pores can become blocked. Even if bathing every day is impossible, splash and rub water over your face, neck, and arms to help wash away the sweat and oils at least once daily.

* **Air out your clothes.** If there isn't enough fresh water to wash your clothes, remove the garments that are closest to your skin, turn them inside out, and lay them in the sun for at least an hour daily to decrease the chances of parasites flourishing in the fabric. Rinse them out in water as often as possible.

* **Inspect your body regularly.** Ask someone to inspect your

body while you're naked once every day, paying careful attention to areas you cannot see. This is the best way to discover signs of hygienic ills (such as rashes) as well as ticks, insects, or other parasites.

* Shave your underarm hair to diminish body odor. Moisten mineral salts, crystal rocks, vegetables, sage, or lemongrass and rub a handful on the area as a deodorant.

((((INSIDER TIP))))

No matter how rugged or basic the conditions of the camp, the producers will usually provide an area to be used for human waste. All cast members are required to use the designated toilet areas rather than the more convenient (but sanitarily unsound) practice of "going in the woods," which could deteriorate the conditions of the camp, and worse, foul water supplies. The production company will also provide sanitary napkins and some means of washing hands. All reality contestants must wash their hands after every "restroom" visit.

Burns

First-degree burns are the equivalent of mild sunburn. Second-degree burns cause blistering in the area. Third-degree burns affect all layers of skin and the underlying nerves and tissues. If you experience second- or third-degree burns while taping the show, a medical team will respond. Use the following strategy to treat first- or minor second-degree burns on your own.

((((INSIDER TIP))))

If you are not provided sunscreen upon your arrival at the reality production site, apply a thin coating of wet mud to your entire body as a substitute. Alternatively, avoid direct sunlight as much as possible.

1) **First-degree burns.**

Keep the area dry and clean. Keep the burned area active to increase blood flow and aid in healing.

2) **Second-degree burns.**

Protect the blisters. Maintain them for at least a day by limiting movement and access to the burned area. Seek medical assistance in removing the dead tissue to avoid infection.

REDUCING CONTAMINATION

A clean wound will heal, but a dirty wound can create a cascade of woe that could lead to tissue loss, excessive scarring, and infection. When treating a wound, adhere to the following principles to guarantee cleanliness and healing:

* **Irrigate the wound with boiled drinking water.** The water best flushes out contaminants when delivered with some pressure, so pour from a foot or so above it.

* **Remove all foreign bodies and materials.** Glass, gravel, and other foreign particles must be removed. Irrigate (as above), scrub, pinch the offending particle, and remove.

* **Assure good blood flow to the injured area.** As long as there is good blood flow into the wound, and there is no obstruction (foreign body, abscess, blood clot, dead tissue) that would limit free blood flow, the body should take care of any microscopic invaders.

* **Do not stitch a wound yourself.** There is always a temptation to "stitch up" a wound, but this is a very bad idea while out in the field. You are much better off with a large scar than with a severe soft tissue infection that remains undrained.

* **Inspect the wound twice a day.** Check for signs of tissue infection, including:

  * Redness
  * Increased pain
  * Swelling
  * Heat
  * Loss of function
  * Red streaking from the wound

  Other general symptoms of infection include fever, chills, and swollen lymph nodes in the groin and armpits. Notify the producers, who should arrange for you to receive professional medical attention.

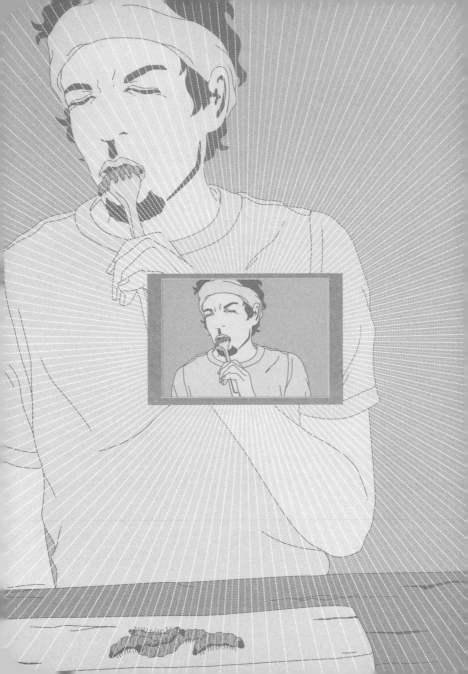

CHAPTER 5

CHALLENGE SKILLS

Many reality shows confront contestants with any number of gruelling physical challenges. When it comes to winning the sponsor-of-the-day's new car, a trip to Ibiza, or a brief visit from a family member, your best chance for success is to know the logistics and strategies behind the challenges.

Producers and their teams spend hours dreaming up new ways to push the envelope: new bugs to eat, new heights from which to dangle, and new fears to face. (And the network's lawyers spend as much time determining the potential claims this envelope-pushing could expose them to.) The best and the brightest reality stars know that nothing they will be challenged to do will hurt them . . . at least not permanently.

Knowing that the stunts you're facing have the network's risk-assessment team's seal of approval should take the edge off your fear. And if that is not enough of an upper hand, the techniques in this chapter will give you and your alliance that extra nudge toward the finish line.

Here's one more hint: Keep your eyes open, because occasionally crewmembers (un)knowingly hold the keys to that shiny new car.

HOW TO OVERCOME FEAR

Whether you find yourself navigating the roof of a rain-soaked taxicab making an abrupt turn at 35 mph (56 kph), dangling 150 feet (45 m) over a bay, or swimming in a tank with small but hungry mako sharks in order to win your loot, you will be dealing with one common denominator—fear of the unknown. If you had faced a tankful of sharks in the past, you probably wouldn't be as afraid this time around. But even seasoned thrill seekers with some prior experience overcoming fear can be sure that prime-time producers will have a curveball (or at least some sharp knives) to throw at you. The only way to advance to the next round is to keep your wits about you and manage your fear, says stuntwoman Danielle Burgio.

1) Place your trust in the stunt coordinators and their expertise and equipment.

You do not have the time—or the experience—to second-guess the setup in front of you. However, for your own peace of mind, double check the equipment you've been given. Look for rusted or unlocked snap-hooks, duct tape, or frayed or brittle rope or wire. Check that any harness you are strapped to is securely fastened around you, and be sure that any rope, bungee, or wire attached to the harness is also attached to a solid anchor.

2) Talk to the coordinators and their assistants.

Connect with the stunt coordinators on a human level before the stunt begins. Make small talk with them—ask them about their

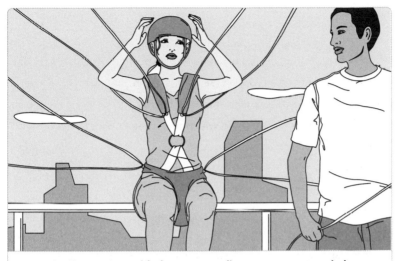

Create a rapport with the stunt coordinator to ease your mind.

experiences on other stunt sets, and tell them about your family and other things that matter to you. This will help you feel comfortable giving them control of the stunt—and help them recognize that you have people back home who care about your safety. Be aware, however, that you are ultimately responsible for looking out for your own emotional and physical health.

((((INSIDER TIP))))

The chances of serious injury or death from a failed stunt on a reality show are much slimmer than television viewers may be led to believe. Aside from the professional stunt coordinators and their assistants who test, check, retest, and recheck a stunt, the network's risk-assessment team will keep a lid on reality producers' desires to "push the envelope."

3)   **Use breathing exercises to remain in control.**

If you can control your breath, then you are in control of your body. Breathe in through your nose and out your mouth. Control the speed and duration of each breath to help your mind focus on your body's movements.

((((INSIDER TIP))))

There is usually a "stop-down" (meaning the cameras stop recording) on the set of a reality show right after the host presents you with a challenge but before you actually perform it. During this period, you will be fitted with the rig (stunt equipment, harnesses, helmet cameras, etc.), a producer will explain the rules of the stunt, and a stunt safety expert will explain the safety equipment and answer all of your questions.

Try to gain valuable information during the briefing. For instance, ask whether anyone has been successful in completing the stunt during the tests, and if so, what the fastest time was. This will help you pace yourself. Ask if everyone who's attempted the stunt finished it. If the answer is no, ask what they did wrong. You might not receive an answer, but if you do, you'll have valuable insight into how to perform the stunt correctly.

4)   **Hope for the best, but prepare for the worst.**

As you examine the stunt before you, you should acknowledge everything that can go wrong and what you would do to right a mishap. This will serve to prime your reflexes for an accident. Just prior to and during a stunt, however, think only about a positive outcome.

5)   **Commit.**

Once you are focused on the task, go through with it. Don't look back. Don't second-guess yourself. Don't question your motives at this stage in the game. Just perform the task at hand.

HOW TO EAT ALMOST ANYTHING

The successful reality star knows that winning involves the mind, body . . . and stomach. It's one thing to face an angry ex, but it's quite another to face a plate of squirming larvae. Careful preparation and strong mental fortitude will allow you to achieve seemingly impossible control over your gag reflexes as you eat your way through a bowl of bull's testicles and move on to victory. The key to successfully eating anything? It's all in the mind. Here are the mental strategies games producer Christopher Lore uses to taste-test his gruesome eating challenges.

Preparation

1) **Empty your stomach.**

Prior to the competition, extend your index finger down your throat to activate your gag reflex and regurgitate any food from your stomach. An eating challenge is much easier to pull off when you are actually hungry. Additionally, your saliva glands will secrete more saliva on an empty stomach, which will make swallowing a handful of mealworms or cow cheeks much easier.

((((INSIDER TIP))))

Anticipation is half the battle when it comes to eating contests, so don't be surprised if there is a fake "technical glitch" that holds up taping right after the gruesome challenge is presented, but before you are given the go-ahead to start eating.

Nothing you are asked to eat will kill you.

2)   Focus on mundane matters.

The mental challenge of eating anything is seriously handicapped if you keep your focus on how disgusting the meal will be—it is much easier to maintain "mind over stomach" in short bursts. Waiting becomes fearful anticipation, and fear triggers the gag reflex. As you stand over a blended pint of sheep's placenta, casually discuss the weather, a sporting event, or other banal matters with your fellow contestants.

3)   Remember that what you're about to eat won't kill you.

Humans are omnivores, and are thus capable of digesting a remarkably wide variety of foods. Eating challenges typically focus on proteins, which may even help you build or sustain your energy throughout other challenges. What you are about to eat has sustained humans at some place and time.

4)   Keep an open mind.

Harness your adventurous spirit—you may find that the disgusting items actually taste pretty good, especially if they are cooked. Certain insects and grubs, in particular, can have a rich, nutty taste that many people enjoy (see "Tastes Like Chicken," on page 150).

Eating

1)   Breathe through your mouth to suppress your olfactory sensors.

The brain processes both smell and taste by combining the stimuli and recognizing or reacting to the flavors. You do not need a sense of smell to recognize sweet, sour, or salty flavors; however, more complex flavors (such as strawberries or maggots) require both taste and smell stimuli to be recognized. As a result, the rancid odor of mealworms, larvae, cockroaches, and unseasoned animal parts may activate your gag reflex as you prepare to eat. Close your nasal passages and breathe in and out through your mouth.

2)   Visualize alternative foodstuffs.

Picture a food that is similar in size, shape, texture, and flavor to the fare you are about to consume (see "Tastes Like Chicken," on page

150). For example, imagine that a cockroach is a walnut to prepare yourself for the crunch. Imagine that ants are lemon drops to prepare yourself for the citrus taste of their metasoma, the rear section that contains its stomach and rectum.

3)   Generate additional saliva in your mouth.

To dilute any rancid or bitter tastes, and to facilitate swallowing, use the following technique to generate extra saliva:

- Imagine you are holding a lemon.
- Stare at the dimples in the lemon peel.
- Now imagine that you have cut a wedge out of the citrus with a sharp knife.
- Visualize that you are squeezing the lemon.
- Take a bite out of the imaginary wedge.

((((INSIDER TIP))))

Eating challenges are carefully sanitized (and the food is sometimes secretly boiled or microwaved). All bugs are farm raised to avoid any possibility of transferring illness or infection. A network's risk-management team has carefully studied the menu, and several producers will have already eaten samples of the feast that awaits you. The plate of bloody offal may look and smell disgusting, but it will be safe to eat.

4)   Swallow quickly, but not too quickly.

Trying to swallow food without chewing will trigger your gag reflex. However, overchewing the food will cause you to dwell on the texture, which may hinder your ability to get (and keep) the provisions down. As a general rule, swallow anything 1/2 inch (1.5 cm) or smaller without chewing. If the food is larger, bite it into 1/2-inch (1.5 cm) pieces before swallowing.

5)   **Repeat steps 2 through 4 as you move to your next course.**

((((INSIDER TIP))))

Before auditioning for the show, confer with your doctor to establish your list of allergies. Your life (and victory) may depend on your listing everything that you are allergic to or simply would rather not eat when you fill out the application form. Be creative—the show's producers certainly will be.

TASTES LIKE CHICKEN

Use the following guide to prepare yourself for the smell, texture, and flavor of various reality foodstuffs. Once you know what an object really tastes like, you can imagine something familiar and similar when it comes time to eat it.

Item	Taste	Virtual Flavor
Maggot	Very little taste; overpowering smell; distinct pop when chewed	Wheat gluten

Item	Taste	Virtual Flavor
Pig's rectum	Salty, fatty taste; extremely rubbery	Dark chicken meat or squid
Waxworms (bee moth larvae)	Faintly buttery, salty taste	Popcorn
Nightcrawlers	Bitter, with a raw oyster texture	Sour gummy worms
Sheep eyes	Rancid, salty taste; rubbery texture that bursts when chewed	Hard-boiled egg with gefilte-fish jelly

HOW TO DEAL WITH BEING BURIED ALIVE

Buried alive. The spine tingles at the mere thought of a living body prematurely interred. Add in the related fears of suffocation, claustrophobia, and the dark, and you have a very potent primal fear indeed. Aside from the horror, there are several practical reasons producers have buried so many contestants alive: It is a simple challenge to set up and film, which is important for keeping a production on track and on budget, and it is an easy challenge to edit, since it primarily consists of nightscope images of contestants whimpering, crying, and talking to themselves. The unprepared contestant may easily go mad underground, but not if he or she understands the role that imagination plays in the challenge. Psychologist Dr. Barry Goldstein and hypnotist Sebastian Black agree that you must control your focus when underground.

1) **Enter the box and begin self-soothing talk.**
Tell yourself that you will be fine.

2) **Explore the box.**
Feel around the box with your appendages to obtain a clear mental picture of your new surroundings.

3) **When being covered by earth, begin to hum.**
The random and unfamiliar sounds of rocks hitting the top of the box may throw your brain into a tailspin. Take control of the

sounds your brain is processing. Hum a familiar or even a newly composed tune to drown out the external sounds.

4)   **Tap your heels against the bottom of the box.**
Focus on the sensations in your feet, legs, hips, torso, and arms as your feet hit the box. The vibration, touch, and rhythm generated by your feet will provide your brain with stimuli other than those of your dark, confining, muffled surroundings. Change the rhythm of your tapping if you think you feel something crawling on you or otherwise entering your space and disturbing your peace of mind.

air pipe

Control your fear by exploring the box with your hands and feet.

5) | **Visualize all of your relatives.**

As you wait to be excavated, recreate a visual picture of each of your relatives, from head to toe. Imagine every inch and every element of each of your family members. Think about their height, hair color, facial blemishes, eye color, smile, eyebrow curves, and so forth. Begin with your closest relatives (spouse, offspring, parents, etc.) and move to your furthest relatives (great-uncles, great-aunts, and second cousins once removed).

OF SOUND MIND

The human brain creates far more fear than any external stimulus. When an ape hears a noise in the jungle, its brain reacts to the stimulus and then quickly forgets about it. When humans hear a noise in the jungle, our brains spend the next hour trying to figure out what the sound was.

When you are introduced to a new situation (for instance, being placed in a small pitch-black box, and then buried under several feet of earth), your brain, being unfamiliar with the new stimuli, will overcompensate with hypersensitive interpretations of sounds and sights. You may begin to hallucinate. You may begin to hear and misinterpret sounds that are barely audible. If you can generate stimuli—humming, tapping, or singing—for your brain to interpret and quickly let go of (like the ape), you stand a much better chance of overcoming a potentially terrifying situation.

HOW TO COMPETE IN WATER

When considering all of the challenges that might be in store, it's only natural for a reality contestant to become preoccupied with eating insects or facing terrifying heights. Contestants might be tempted to overlook one entire set of more common challenges—those taking place in water. Water challenges can take a variety of forms, including swimming races, endurance contests, underwater scavenger hunts, and even breath-holding contests. Producers and the networks' risk-assessment teams will try out all challenges beforehand, but the unpredictability of water makes the potential for injury very real. Your best strategy for success in the water is to relax. Let your body work with the water and thus against your opponents. Eric Fattah, a world record–holding free diver, and master swimmer Dennis Tesch offer up the following advice for aquatic success.

Swimming

1) **Relax.**

Relax your body as you kick and stroke through the water. Move your limbs rapidly, but keep them loose and tension-free. Most people think that if you want to swim faster you must tense up your muscles and go as hard and strong as you can. Particularly in the ocean, but also in still bodies of water (pools, lakes, etc.), the opposite is true. A tight chest and tensed body will also limit your lung capacity and use more energy.

2)   Keep your mind focused on your goal, but keep aware of your body's responsiveness at all times.

3)   If you are swimming to a specific location, maintain a constant, easy pace.

Don't go hard at the beginning, especially when you are faced with a long-distance swim. Swim at a pace that's the aerobic equivalent of a fast walk or jog as opposed to a hard run. Your time will be slower if you are constantly speeding up and slowing down. Roll onto your back and use an easier stroke if you feel yourself tiring. Even if you fall behind, stay steady. If you need a burst of energy at the end, you'll have it, due to your constant and comfortable pace.

Packing Your Lungs

Holding your breath is a science and an art. Use these steps to learn how to "pack" your lungs, a technique that will allow you to hold up to 1 gallon (4 liters) of extra air—and add 30 seconds or more to your underwater time. This edge will enhance your ability to compete in breath-holding competitions or contests that involve retrieving objects underwater.

1)   Learn to force air into your lungs.

• Close your mouth and hold your nose.

• Force air from your lungs into your mouth, expanding your cheeks.

• Now squeeze your cheeks, forcing the air back into your lungs. Make sure the air is going into your lungs, not into your stomach, by forcing your diaphragm to accept the air into your lungs by sucking in your abdomen.

- Repeat these steps until you are comfortable pushing air into your lungs.

2) **Learn the difference between "sucking" air and "inhaling" air.**

- Using a drinking straw, *suck* air into your mouth (imagine that you are drinking a milkshake). Your esophagus remains closed, and the suction for drawing the air is created by your cheeks, mouth, and throat.

- Now *inhale* air into your lungs through the straw. Note the difference between sucking air and inhaling air. When sucking air, you primarily used your mouth and throat. When inhaling, you used your chest.

3) **Pack your lungs using the straw for assistance.**

- Inhale air through the straw until your lungs are expanded to their maximum.

- Still using the straw, suck still more air into your mouth.

- Remove the straw. Pack your lungs by squeezing your cheeks to force the air into your lungs (using the exercise you mastered in step 1)

- Continue to pack until your lungs cannot hold any more air, or until you feel discomfort.

4)   **Now do it for real.**

Repeat step 3, but without the drinking straw.

Floating and Treading

When you need to tread water in a challenge, avoid using the standard flutter kick. Kicking your legs as you would in a freestyle kick keeps you afloat, but it also uses much more energy than the more efficient techniques that follow.

1)   **Breaststroke Kick.**

Kick both legs simultaneously like a frog. Turn your knees and feet out (so that the soles of your feet face each other). Kick out and up. Skull your arms. Alternate this style with the Eggbeater (below) to best conserve energy when treading water.

2)   **Eggbeater Kick.**

Circle your feet in alternating directions. If your right foot circles counter-clockwise, your left should circle clockwise. Skull your arms straight out to your sides and straight back.

((((INSIDER TIP))))

Stay calm! Chances are, you will be confronted with a surprise as you swim—a fish could brush your leg, an inflatable prop may be triggered just as you swim by, or snakes may be released into the water. Don't let your nerves get to you. Panic will cause an increase in your heart rate, which will reduce your overall stamina.

BREASTSTROKE KICK

EGGBEATER KICK

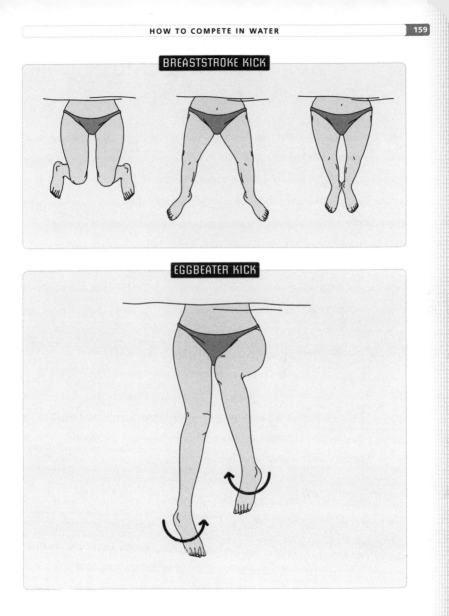

HOW TO RAPPEL DOWN A MOUNTAIN

You can be certain that any reality show with physical challenges will involve some type of rappel—and thus, a great opportunity to build a story arc for your character. With some invention (declaring early on that you have a paralyzing fear of heights), some character development (reluctantly offering to climb a small rock to reach a berry bush), and some skill (see below), you can concoct a trial-and-tribulation story that is a producer's dream. Expert climber Sky Beck recommends that you trust your equipment, lean back, and never let go of your brake rope—unless you really need to build up your victory moment.

1) | **Double-check all of your equipment.**

Official stunt coordinators will secure you in your sit harness and attach you to an anchor with the appropriate equipment (see "Rappelling Equipment" on page 164). While you should trust all of your equipment and the coordinators, always double-check your connections for your own peace of mind.

2) | **Grasp the brake side of the rope with your dominant hand.**

The stunt coordinators will suit you up so that the brake side of the rope will be in your dominant hand. Pull down on the brake rope, and *do not let go.* Though you will have backups to catch you, letting go of the brake side of the rope will cause you to fall and potentially lose a challenge.

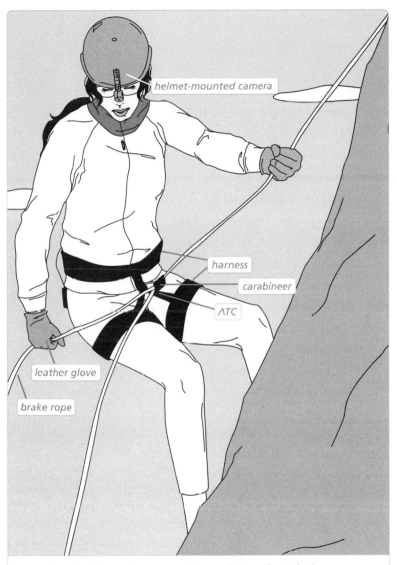

Lean back in your harness and do not let go of your brake rope.

3) **Place your feet on the edge of the rappelling surface.**

Place your nondominant hand on the rope in front of you to guide and stabilize your descent. With the balls of your feet on the edge of the rappelling surface, apply the brake fully by pulling the brake rope down and away from you. Lean all of your weight back into the sit harness.

4) **Begin your descent.**

Slowly release a bit of tension from the brake side rope while simultaneously walking a few steps down the vertical face. Lean back as you step. Your feet will be flat against the rappelling surface and your body will be at a 30- to 45-degree angle to the surface.

5) **Continue your descent until you are on the ground.**

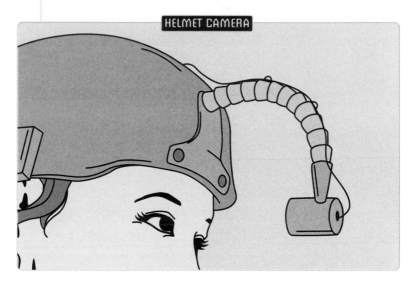

HELMET CAMERA

HOW TO MASTER A HELMET-MOUNTED CAMERA

Helmet-mounted cameras are very popular for taping reality-show action sequences. Up to three cameras are affixed to a safety helmet, each offering a different vantage. The usual configuration, though, is two cameras: one aimed at your face, the other aimed outward, to show your viewpoint.

Typically, these helmets are "one size fits all," which means that contestants never have a truly comfortable fit. To further add to the discomfort, you must also wear a heavy fanny pack that carries the tape deck. The most notable drawback, however, is the fact that no one looks very good through the fixed-camera position of the helmet cam—potentially affecting the viewers' perception of you, and thus your ability to spin a sixteenth minute of fame.

But while the cameras simply cannot be avoided, they can be manipulated for more flattering angles. Here's what to do:

* **Move your entire head when looking around.** Helmet-mounted cameras tend to make the subject appear wild-eyed because the face stays motionless in the television frame, accentuating the movement of the eyes.

* **Move the camera.** This can't always be done, but often the camera facing you is on a flexible arm that can be adjusted. Once the tech crew is satisfied with the way the camera is mounted, give it a little nudge. Since the recorder is in the fanny pack you are wearing, nobody will notice that the angle is unusable until it is too late.

RAPPELLING EQUIPMENT

The basic climbing—and recording—equipment will generally include:

* ATC or "Air Traffic Controller." A metal cup divided in half and supported by a sheathed cable. ATC allows you to create the friction you need to control the speed of your descent.

* Carabineer or "Beener." A locking clip that attaches your harness to the ATC.

* Harness. A device that fits around both legs and up and around your pelvis. Sit harnesses are designed to support your weight—in conjunction with the other equipment—in a seated posture.

* Climbing rope.

* Leather gloves.

* Lav microphone. Microphone that attaches to your chest, with a wire running to a separate transmitter. It will record any sounds you emit as you approach and descend.

* Helmet-mounted camera. Camera that both protects your head from injury and records your facial reactions as you repel, panic, or fall (see "How to Master a Helmet-Mounted Camera," on page 163).

* Secondary rope or bungee. Depending on the height of your descent, a secondary security rope or bungee may be attached to your harness to protect your body—but not your integrity—should you fall.

HOW TO MANEUVER A TEAM THROUGH AN OBSTACLE COURSE OR MAZE

Obstacle courses and mazes appear frequently as challenges in reality shows, and for good reason—they are rife with action, they force character interaction, and they end with clearly defined results. But success in completing an obstacle course does not directly correlate with the diameter of your biceps or how quickly you can run a 10K. Rather, according to security trainer Shawn Engbrecht, victory depends on your ability to assess the landscape, organize as a team, conserve energy, and generally focus on each step along the way. Your survival, or at least your chance to eat a real meal or win a new SUV, relies on it.

Obstacle Strategies

When confronting obstacles of all types, your greatest challenge is to work as a team. Most likely—unless producers are planning a "sell out your teammates" plot twist—you will all have to cross the finish line in order to secure victory. The following obstacle-specific strategies will provide you with an edge on the competition.

1) River crossing.

   If you do not have a rope to help you cross the river, find the nearest and narrowest place to cross. Wade or swim across with another person. If you are supplied with a rope, use a technique called *ferrying* to offset the current. With one end of the rope in hand, send your team's best swimmer far enough upstream so that when she swims across the river the current will push her roughly to the desired landing zone on the other side. Your advance "scout" and your team should anchor the rope at both ends to a tree or rock on opposite sides of the river. Each member of the team can then use the rope to travel hand over hand across the river. The final member of the team to cross should untie the rope from the starting point; the teammates who've already crossed can pull him across to the opposite shore.

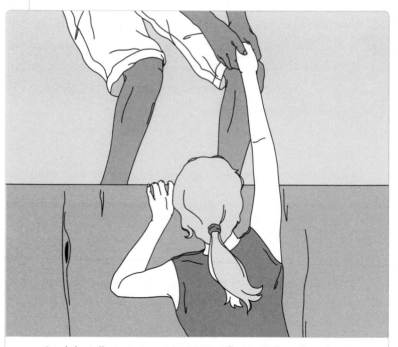

Send the tallest, strongest teammates first to pull up the others.

2)   Vertical wall.

Run directly at the wall and jump up, hitting the wall feet first. Press up with your feet, and extend your hands to the top of the wall. *Do not hang on the wall.* Use your upward and forward momentum to pull yourself to the top (or to your teammate's waiting hand). Pull up with your arms, and bicycle peddle with your feet to scramble to the top. Note: Send your tallest and strongest teammate to climb the wall first—once he's made it he can straddle the top and extend a helping hand to the remaining team members.

3)   Balance beam.

Focus on the beam about 12 to 15 feet in front of you—your body will instinctively go to your focal point. Move quickly across the beam and keep a forward momentum. Do not look down. If you fall, do not straddle the beam.

4)   Cargo net.

Identify the anchor points on the cargo net; these are the sections of rope that are tied to solid surfaces, generally above, below, and to both sides. Begin to climb the net on a line nearest an anchor point, the most stable section of the net. Climb hand over hand—as you would with a single hanging rope—up one section of rope. Use a rapid bicycle-peddling motion with your feet on the horizontal rope lines to increase speed. The faster your arms move, the faster your feet will follow.

Maze Skills

Use the following strategies to navigate a maze with your teammates.

1) Identify a navigational landmark.

Mazes or rope courses often are constructed with high walls or within heavily forested areas. Prior to entering the challenge, look for high mountain or volcano peaks or uniquely colored or styles of trees which might be viewed from within the labyrinth. As you run through the maze, check your relation to the landmark to keep your sense of direction.

2) Count your steps and track your turns.

Assign the task of counting steps to one teammate and the task of tracking turns to another. When you are in a maze, your success depends on your ability to backtrack quickly and remember where you have already been. This technique will keep you from becoming disoriented.

3) Rotate scouting responsibility among teammates.

Don't expend energy unnecessarily when navigating longer labyrinths. One member of the group should move ahead of the rest to scout an area and then return to take the group through. Rotate this responsibility from teammate to teammate to conserve and balance the energy of the group—particularly when your group has not been eating regular meals.

((((**INSIDER TIP**))))

When walking through a labyrinth, place your right hand on the nearest wall to your right and follow it to the end of the maze. This strategy may add time to your navigation, but you will avoid moving in circles.

4)   Assign rally points.

As you move through the maze, select several rally points along the way. Mark the ground in some way, or take note of an unusual tree branch or discoloring on the wall. Be sure that everyone in your group is aware of them. If your team gets split up, any trailing members should go back to the nearest rally point and stay put. The leading members of the team will return to that point to collect the stragglers.

HOW TO GET HELP FROM THE CREW

This section contains the key to one of reality television's deepest, darkest secrets: If you are lucky, you might find some unexpected help from a most unlikely source—a member of the crew. Crew members are fired on the spot if they are caught assisting the cast in any way, and yet they sometimes do so anyway. Help from the crew can take the form of cigarettes or breakfast bars, but it will most likely materialize as a hint in the middle of a game (such as a puzzle or a scavenger hunt). There are ethical considerations when a contestant seeks assistance from the crew, but if you are comfortable with cheating (and are willing to forfeit your winnings if you are caught), the sources for this section (who request anonymity) offer up the following strategy for getting the inside scoop.

1) Establish a relationship with the crew.

The crews on reality shows are instructed to wander around you as if they don't exist. They will avoid making eye contact, and they will never speak to you unless they absolutely have to. You don't have to play by the same rules. From the very first day, be considerate of crew members in your vicinity. If you are walking through a jungle, you might say to the camera person, "Let me know if I'm walking too quickly." Thank the audio assistant each time he changes your battery or sets up your mic. Don't worry if they respond to you in a stone-faced manner—your courtesy will not go unnoticed.

2) **Flirt.**

Almost every case of a crew member helping a contestant involves a mutual attraction. A spark of attraction between you and a crew member will greatly increase your chances that he will assist you.

((((INSIDER TIP))))

While attraction is the primary impetus for a crew member risking his job for you, sometimes basic kindness comes into play. If the crew feels like the producers are unfairly picking on a contestant, especially a contestant who has shown him- or herself to be a decent person, they may take pity and help you out.

Flirt or otherwise secretly bond with a crew member to encourage him to help you—be it in the form of food or a hint during a challenge.

3) **Use slight facial expressions to ask for help.**

To escape detection, you will have to ask for help through the tiniest of facial expressions. Make eye contact with the crew member with whom you have formed a bond, and then make a slight quizzical expression that implies, "I have no idea what I should do here." Roll your eyes, suggesting, "This is pointless." Chances are the crew member will feel the same way about the game, and this shared sense of perspective might encourage the crew member to help you.

4) **Watch for subtle hints.**

The crew member will most often communicate assistance through tiny eye movements. In rarer cases, hints will come through very slight head gestures, so look for barely perceptible nods or head shakes.

((((INSIDER TIP))))

Don't be surprised if the crew members turn their backs on you during crucial game moments, a safeguard some shows enforce when the producers don't want to take any chances that someone might receive a hint.

5) **Protect your source.**

Never reveal either the hint or its source to *anyone*. The crew member who broke ranks to help you put his job at risk and can be fired or suffer a damaged reputation if he's discovered even after the show is over. You may also put yourself in jeopardy if you admit to having cheated on the show, especially if you continued to advance to the next rounds.

THE DIRECT APPROACH

In some circumstances, you can ask the crew for help in a direct manner, using words instead of gestures. This strategy works particularly well if you are on a show where a crew is assigned to each contestant—for instance, a race-type show. Under such circumstances, you and your crew will inevitably develop a bond fostered through constant proximity. There is also a good chance that the field producer will get so caught up in the competition and the desire to be paired with a finalist that she will feed you information. (This will happen while the rest of the production crew is on a break or asleep.)

If you are unable to get the producer on your side, attempt to sway the crew. Approach the crew during a tape change, when batteries are replaced and there is no chance of being recorded (and no chance the field producer can overhear the conversation). Apologize for being so lost and causing them to work so hard. After several such apologies they may give you a nudge in the right direction—especially if it is a hint that gives everyone a bit more rest.

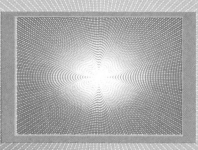

EPILOGUE

BACK TO REALITY

Faster than you can imagine, your show will end. After some hugs and maybe even a wrap party, you will have to return to a life without cameras and craft-service tables. It will all seem like a dream: One day you are a star, with segment producers and technicians following your every action, and the next day it's back to work and making your own bed.

To further add to the surrealism, you aren't allowed to tell anyone what you did or why you were gone because you signed a confidentiality agreement that forces you to keep the whole experience a secret until the show airs. Some reality stars have had to hold their tongues and their newly packed wallets for more than a year while networks adjust their programming schedules.

A gymnast can perform a nearly flawless routine on the parallel bars, only to lose points on a stumbling dismount. The same fate can befall a reality star. Your performance during the postshow interviews and the manner in which you attempt to extend your 15 minutes of fame can make the difference between your reality show adventure being just a bullet point on your resume or the start of a whole new career.

Good luck!

HOW TO SHINE IN A TALK SHOW INTERVIEW

If your reality show was popular, you will be in demand on the network morning news shows. As a new celebrity, you'll want to make the most of this opportunity to extend your time in front of the camera. As producer Mindy Moore explains, trust the segment producer, keep a smile on your face, and follow these tips for handling the interview.

1) **Follow the instructions of the segment producer.**

A segment producer will greet you when you arrive at the studio. The segment producer will conduct a preinterview with you, give you the rough list of questions you should be prepared for, and even go over your responses.

2) **Avoid taboos.**

• Do not touch the hosts.

• Unless specifically instructed to do so, do not call the hosts by their first names.

• Never look at the camera. Only the hosts are allowed to make "direct" contact with the home audience.

3) **Smile.**

As soon as you see the camera's red light go on, put a smile on your face and keep it there for the entire interview. A smile helps to maintain the energy level (which will keep viewers tuned in). It will also help to mute some of the barbs and harsh questions the host might plan on throwing at you.

4) **Answer the host's questions with two-sentence responses.** Shorter answers will cause the interview to seem truncated (and won't give the host time to scan notes for the next question), and longer answers will make you sound like you are rambling.

WATCHING YOURSELF ON THE SHOW

As you gather with friends and family to watch your starring role, be ready for some embarrassment. You will be prepared for the uncomfortable moments you remember (the drunken nights, angry outbursts, and blooming romances). However, the moments you don't see coming will cause the most blushing. Here's a rundown of what you can expect.

* **The events portrayed might not be as you remember them.** Producers and editors need to create an exciting television show from your experiences. Music and editing may transform what you remember as an innocent moment into a scene of high comedy or drama. Do not be surprised if a minor, barely noticed misunderstanding is amplified into a major confrontation when the show airs. Many events and conversations that explain your actions and present you in a more favorable light will not make the show at all.

* **You may not recognize yourself.** The cameras were rolling continuously, and from the hundreds of hours of tape recorded,

some shots may be lifted out of context, presenting implications you never intended. For instance, while you may have rolled your eyes in a good-natured reaction to a joke during a break in the action, that same shot might be used as a sarcastic, dismissive reaction to another character's emotional plea. Scratching your face can be edited to look like you are wiping away tears.

* **Friends might not be friends.** This is probably the most painful moment for reality stars watching their show on the air. You may discover during the broadcast that you were betrayed by a supposed friend.

HOW TO EXTEND YOUR 15 MINUTES OF FAME

Whether you win or lose your reality show, the real money comes in how you play your postgame. Play your cards right, and you can spin your momentary fame into an exciting new career. Just because you are out of the limelight doesn't mean that you are not a valuable commodity. Build on the character you ultimately became—at the hands of editors and producers—and play that role to the best of your abilities. Any of the following strategies will help you enjoy at least a 16th minute of fame after the show.

* Move to New York or Los Angeles.

* Star in the next installment of the reality show in which you just participated.

* Write a book.

* Do a cameo in a situational comedy or television commercial.

* Announce the breakup of your reality-show relationship.

* Run for a public office.

* Pose nude.

* Appear on a cast reunion special.

* Allow a television network to film your wedding.

* Give speeches on college campuses.

* Land a role on a soap opera.

* Dramatically alter your appearance by losing a significant amount of weight, getting breast implants, or having cosmetic surgery.

* Crash celebrity parties and be photographed with them.

* Become a special correspondent on a tabloid television show.

* Participate in a celebrity boxing match.

* Become a morning-show radio DJ.

* Open a restaurant or bar.

* Start your own line of clothing.

* Start a band.

* Become the national spokesperson for a nonprofit organization.

* Cohost a cable game show.

* Provide on-screen testimonials for infomercial products.

APPENDIX: REALITY TV GLOSSARY

A.D.: Assistant director.

Base camp: An area specifically designated to house the crew and its equipment when shooting on location.

Beauty shots: Shots of animals, nature, or landscapes used to reinforce the location.

Blur: The postproduction process of blurring license plates, faces of individuals who didn't sign release forms, logos of companies that don't have product-placement agreements, nudity, and other elements in the frame that can't be broadcast for legal purposes.

C-47s: Clothespins.

Confessional: An on-camera interview in which the subject looks straight into the lens of the camera.

Confidentiality agreement: A legal document signed by all cast and crew members that threatens penalties in the millions of dollars for disclosing any aspect of the production before the show airs.

Craft service: A table of snacks and drinks for the crew, sometimes off limits to the cast.

Cut-away: An edit away from the person speaking to focus on someone or something else. Usually used to disguise a *pull-up* (see page 183).

D.P.: Director of photography.

DV: Small digital video camera. Very small cameras that are used to provide additional inexpensive angles.

Establishing shot: A shot of a building or environment that establishes the location of the action that follows. Can be a convenient place to present signs or logos for businesses such as jewelers, hotels, or restaurants that provided trade-outs.

Ice cube: A tiny camera, about the size of an ice cube, used for hidden-camera setups and unique camera angles, such as on a helmet cam or affixed to a surfboard. Also called a *pencil cam.*

IFB: A small earpiece that allows producers and directors to communicate with on-screen talent.

ITM (In the Moment): A spontaneous interview, conducted in the heat of the action. Also called an *OTF* (On The Fly).

Jib: A long pole holding a camera that is affixed to a base support. Allows for high-angle shots and sweeping camera movements.

Lav mic (Lavalier microphone): A tiny microphone that is usually clipped to a shirt or tie.

Loop: A technical process whereby a contestant or host's words are re-recorded and then inserted back into the scene (in cases when the location conditions caused poor original recording). Sometimes new lines are added to clarify a scene. Also referred to as ADR, or audio dialog replacement.

Magic hour: A period during dawn and dusk when natural lighting conditions are soft and warm.

Nightvision/Nightscope: Products that permit videotaping in very low-light situations.

P.A.: Production assistant.

Pick-ups: The videotaping of additional material after the primary action has ended. Examples include characters walking in or out of a room, close-ups of hands or objects, or aerial shots.

Post: The editing process. Includes audio mixing.

Product placement: The intentional placement of products or logos within a scene by companies that provide goods, services, or money to the production.

Pull-up: An edit (or series of edits) used to compress time and tighten scenes and interviews by skipping over unwanted material.

Release: A legal document that any person on camera will have to sign, permitting one's name, voice, and likeness to be broadcast.

Saga sell: An extended tease of the entire series, usually placed at the beginning of reality episodes.

Stand-ins: Extras (sometimes low-level production staff members) who attempt stunts or approximate the movements that the contestants will make to allow the director and technical crew to rehearse.

Steadicam: A stabilizing mount, usually worn by a cameraman, that allows smooth, fluid camera moves.

Trade-out: An arrangement between a show and another company for the use of vehicles, cell phones, hotels, restaurants, etc. in exchange for allowing the products and logos to be visible on-screen.

Vanities: Hair and/or makeup.

Video village: A temporary control room, usually hidden from the contestants, where producers and directors can watch the action unfolding and issue commands to the crew.

VO: Voice-over.

ABOUT THE EXPERTS

Chapter 1: Getting on the Show

How to Find Your Show—Sheila Conlin and Katy Wallin operate Mystic Art Pictures, a casting agency in Los Angeles. Together, they cast participants for *Who Wants to Marry My Dad?*, *Paradise Hotel*, and *Mr. Personality*. Sheila is also a producer who just completed a pilot for VH-1, while Katy's background includes casting more than 500 hours of television and more than 70 feature films and telefilms. She also serves on the board of the Casting Society of America.

How to Create Your Application—Sheila Conlin and Katy Wallin.

How to Audition Like an Idol—Nick Bedding is the vice president of adult format promotion at Hollywood Records. He learned the perils of scouting amateur talent firsthand as a judge for STAR 98.7's "Be a Star" contest.

How to Ace a Casting Interview—Patti Wood (www.pattiwood.net) is an international speaker, trainer, and body language expert with more than 20 years of experience. She has written seven books and is a consultant for law enforcement organizations and several major news networks. Erica Rutkin Keswin is an executive director at Russell Reynolds Associates, a global executive recruiting firm, in the global human resources and sports, media, and entertainment practices. Carrie Leonard is a marketing, sales, and business development strategist with more than 13 years of experience in media, entertainment, and consumer products. Since 2000, she has operated an independent consulting practice in New York.

How to Nail the Final Network Interview—Anonymous.

Chapter 2: Strategy Skills

How to Form an Alliance—Suzanne Gooler is the director of organization and leadership development at a major pharmaceutical corporation with more than 11 years of experience in organization development, organization effectiveness, and leadership development in various industries. Dr. Jonathan Butner is a social psychologist at the University of Utah whose primary concentration is analyzing group processes.

How to Fly Under the Radar—Suzanne Gooler.

How to Manipulate Your Competitors—*Influence: The Psychology of Persuasion* by Robert B. Cialdini, regents' professor of psychology at Arizona State University. Dr. Jonathan Butner.

How to Display Emotion on Cue—Drucie McDaniel is an acting coach, director, and actor with a 20-year career in film, television, and theater.

How to Give an On-Camera Interview—Anonymous.

How to Use Alcohol to Your Advantage—Kathy Wetherell was a producer for *Road Rules*, *The Real World/Road Rules Challenge*, *Making the Band*, *Love Cruise*, *The Real World/Road Rules Casting Special*, *The Dating Experiment*, *The Bachelor*, and *Married by America*. Wetherell also produced and directed two seasons of MTV's *Fraternity Life*.

How to Manage Your Enemies—Suzanne Gooler.

How to Make the Most of Losing—Curtis S. Chin is a client-managing partner with Burson-Marsteller, a major public relations and public affairs firm headquartered in New York. He has led a range of communications training workshops for celebrity chefs, Hollywood stars, and political and corporate leaders.

Chapter 3: Relationship Skills

How to Read a Bachelor or Bachelorette's Body Language—Patti Wood.

How to Make the Most of Your Date—Eve Hogan (www.evehogan.com) is the relationship advisor for DreamMates.com and the author of several books, including *Intellectual Foreplay* and *Virtual Foreplay*. She has appeared as a relationship expert on *The Other Half*, the *Iyanla Show*, and the Lifetime network. Dr. Barry Goldstein is a doctoral psychologist who provides psychological consulting for reality television cast members. He has worked on *Joe Millionaire*, *American Idol*, *Meet My Dad*, and *The Real World*, among others.

How to Discern Whether Your Date Is Actually Wealthy—Patti Stanger, a third generation matchmaker, is the CEO and owner of the Millionaire's Club, a dating service for millionaires.

How to Escape the Microphones—Audio mixer Stacy Hill began her reality television career on *Rescue 911* and has since worked on programs for every broadcast and cable network.

How to Hook Up on Camera—Anonymous.

How to Endear Yourself to the Parents—Eve Hogan.

How to Date Multiple Partners—Kathy Wetherell. Sherry Zimmerman is a family lawyer who, with co-author Rosie Einhorn, wrote two books for Jewish singles, *Talking Tachlis* and *In the Beginning*. She is the author of a dating advice column on www.aish.com and the editor of www.jewishdatingandmarriage.com.

Chapter 4: Survival Skills

How to Make Fire—Mel Deweese is a survival evasion resistance escape instructor who has developed, written, attended, and taught courses around the world to more than 100,000 students, including civilians, naval aviators, and elite Navy SEAL teams.

How to Make a Water Pipeline—Mel Deweese.

How to Build Shelter—Mel Deweese.

How to Catch Food—Mel Deweese.

How to Cook in the Wild—Mel Deweese.

How to Deal with Wild Animals—Russ Smith is the curator of reptiles at the Los Angeles Zoo. Randy Miller is the owner and operator of Randy Miller's Predators in Action (www.predatorsinaction.com), specializing in the stunt-action training of lions, tigers, leopards, cougars, wolves, black and grizzly bears, and all other types of animals. He won the World Stunt Academy Award for his work in the movie *Gladiator*.

How to Treat Minor Medical Conditions—Andrew Michaels, M.D., M.P.H., F.A.C.S., is a mountaineer and trauma surgeon in Portland, Oregon. He has worked as a medic in the Army, an EMT, a flight nurse, an alpine guide, and an Outward Bound instructor. Becky Fee, R.N., C.C.R.N., C.F.R.N., is a mountaineer, horsewoman, adventure racer, backcountry skier, and flight nurse. She lives in Portland, Oregon.

Chapter 5: Challenge Skills

How to Overcome Fear—Danielle Burgio (www.danielleburgio.com) is a stuntwoman who appeared in *Matrix Reloaded*, *Matrix Revolutions*, *Daredevil*, and starred in *The Eliminator*.

How to Eat Almost Anything—Christopher Lore is a theater, film, and television producer who has created and produced the trials, games, and challenges for shows such as *Big Brother*, *Dog Eat Dog*, and *I'm a Celebrity, Get Me Out of Here!*

How to Deal with Being Buried Alive—Dr. Barry Goldstein. Sebastian Black is a master hypnotist who travels the United States performing a stage hypnosis show.

How to Compete in Water—Eric Fattah has been free diving since 1999, and has since claimed six Canadian records and one world record for free diving and breath holding. He is the inventor of Fluid Goggles and the Frenzel-Fattah deep equalizing technique. Dennis Tesch is a master swimmer and coach. He holds a masters degree in sports management.

How to Rappel Down a Mountain—Sky Beck is an expert climber at Black Diamond Equipment in Salt Lake City, Utah.

How to Maneuver a Team Through an Obstacle Course or Maze—Shawn Engbrecht is one of the world's top protection officers. When he is not on operational assignment, he is one of the instructors at the Center for Advanced Security Studies (www.bodyguardschool.com), training and placing world-class bodyguards.

How to Get Help from the Crew—Anonymous.

Epilogue: Back to Reality

How to Shine in a Talk Show Interview—Mindy Moore is an award-winning television producer with a background in news. She was a producer on *Good Morning America* and *The View*, and created and executive-produced the critically acclaimed reality show *The Family* for ABC.

How to Extend Your 15 Minutes of Fame—Anonymous.

ACKNOWLEDGMENTS

JOHN SAADE would like to acknowledge the talented producers and staff of unscripted television, who craft popular entertainment under incredible pressure in a constantly evolving genre, and rarely get the credit they deserve for the quality of the stories they present. To Joe, a true creative genius, for providing an eye-opening education into what a co-author does, and to the incredible Melissa Wagner, who provided an equally eye-opening education into what exactly an editor does (just about everything between the two of them, it turns out). It was an amazing experience working with both of them, as well as with all of the other faceless Quirk people at the other end of the conference calls. He also thanks all of the experts, who provided so much expertise, information, and patience; as well as Jeanne Newman, Lee Rierson, Andrea Wong, and Warren Eallonardo. He sends a special thanks to Brad Cates, who whipped up something that was simply too brilliant to include; to Mom and Dad; and finally, to those he cherishes most: his wife, Laura (the single finest person he knows), and the fantastic Catherine/Jack reality show.

JOE BORGENICHT would like to acknowledge all of the producers of reality television—the new miniseries—because without them we'd still be watching reruns of *Shogun* and *The Stand*. He would also like to thank the experts who lent their knowledge to all of these skills—you are the ones who should be on these shows. Thanks to John, for all of his hard work, insights, and reality mastermind. He would like to thank his editor, Melissa Wagner, for making sense of it all (and never taking a day off). To Pierre

Brogan, for providing the introduction and the lunch. To his brother, Dave, as always, who remains on intimate terms with the prairie. To the constantly amazing team at Quirk, who bring these books to life. And finally to his real reality, Melanie ("The Wife") and Jonah ("The Son").

ABOUT THE AUTHORS

As a reality executive at ABC, **JOHN SAADE** developed and oversaw production on *The Bachelor*, *The Mole*, *Extreme Makeover*, *Making the Band*, and *Houston Medical*. He is currently developing a number of reality shows and specials. He lives in Los Angeles with his family.

JOE BORGENICHT is a writer/producer and avid reality connoisseur. In between episodes of the latest shows, Joe has co-written *The Action Hero's Handbook*, *The Action Heroine's Handbook*, *The Baby Owner's Manual*, and *Undercover Golf*. He continues to create his own reality in Salt Lake City, with his wife and son.